AUTISM
ABRACADABRA

AUTISM ABRACADABRA

Seven Magic Ingredients
to Help Develop Your Child's
Interactive Attention Span

Kate C. Wilde

Jessica Kingsley Publishers
London and Philadelphia

First published in Great Britain in 2022 by Jessica Kingsley Publishers
An imprint of Hodder & Stoughton Ltd
An Hachette Company

1

The Son-Rise Program® is a registered trademark of Barry
Neil Kaufman and Susan Marie Kaufman.

The Autism Treatment Center of America® is a Trademark
of The Option Institute and Fellowship.

A CIP catalogue record for this title is available from the
British Library and the Library of Congress

ISBN 978 1 78775 751 6
eISBN 978 1 78775 752 3

Printed and bound in United States by Integrated Books International

Jessica Kingsley Publishers' policy is to use papers that are natural,
renewable and recyclable products and made from wood grown in sus-
tainable forests. The logging and manufacturing processes are expected to
conform to the environmental regulations of the country of origin.

Jessica Kingsley Publishers
Carmelite House
50 Victoria Embankment
London EC4Y 0DZ

www.jkp.com

To my dearest Jade Adina Hogan
We built magical wonderlands together
This book could not have happened without you
So grateful to be living this life with you
I love you

Acknowledgments

To my teachers Samahria Lyte Kaufman (Co-Creator of the Son-Rise Program), Barry Neil Kaufman (Co-Creator of the Son-Rise Program), Bryn Hogan (Master Son-Rise Program Teacher) and William Hogan (Master Son-Rise Program Teacher). In gratitude for your wisdom, guidance, time, knowledge, love and vision. I am standing on your shoulders.

To every child and adult on the spectrum I have worked with, for allowing me to see your spirit, intelligence, kindness and daring. I am in awe of the way you live your lives.

Huge thanks to Raun K. Kaufman (Master Son-Rise Program Teacher, Co-Creator of the Autism Crisis Turnaround), my dear colleague and lifelong friend. Thank you for the big-hearted way you supported me with this book, helping me structure it, giving me feedback and suggesting content. You helped me make it into a greater version of itself. Thank you from the bottom of my heart.

To my mum, Elizabeth McCormick. You are my rock, my super supporter and champion. Thank you for always being there for me, for reading everything I give you and giving me the confidence to begin and keep writing.

To my editor Elaine Leek, thank you for giving me your valuable time and insights and catching all the dyslexic mistakes my brain can't see. To Jessica Kingsley Publishers for publishing all my books, especially to my commissioning editors Sarah Hamlin and Lisa Clark.

Contents

My Story

I was 13 when I decided to work with children on the autism spectrum. The catalyst and inspiration for this decision was a movie called *Son-Rise: A Miracle of Love*. I watched this with my twin sister, Nicky. Watching this movie was the beginning of everything. It was my first introduction to autism and I was completely intrigued and fascinated by it. I became the kind of teenager who only read the Cliffs Notes for her school-assigned books because she was too busy reading other books on child development. It was also my first introduction to the concept that love and acceptance are the most powerful forces for healing and change. Luckily, my 13-year-old brain was still open enough to receive the powerful truth of this message.

The movie *Son-Rise: A Miracle of Love* is the real-life story of Samahria and Barry Neil Kaufman, whose son was diagnosed with severe autism and an IQ of under 30 at 18 months, and their journey to help him. In the 1970s, there was little available in the way of autism treatments as at that time only one in 10,000 children were thought to be affected. At that time, harsh behavior-modification techniques, including electric shock, were being used to treat severe autism, and this was not something they wanted for their son. The Kaufmans searched for help for their son and were told repeatedly that autism was a lifelong condition and that there was no chance for their son to lead a normal life, or even learn very basic skills to take care of himself. Doctors advised institutionalization. Instead of going with the treatments they were offered by professionals, they decided to work with their son themselves. They took a very different approach from the mainstream thinking and attitudes of that time. Instead of viewing their son's unique behaviors of hand flapping and rocking as a tragic sign of his "terrible disorder," they took a different view.

They decided to see him as a gift in their life. They decided to approach him not with disapproval or fear, but with love and acceptance. Instead of forcing him to conform to their world, they decided to "join"[1] him in his. They saw his repetitive behaviors as a doorway into his world, so when he flapped his hands, they flapped theirs. When he rocked back and forth, they rocked with him. By joining him in his world, they were able to make a connection between them. They worked with their son 12 hours a day for three and a half years. Today he shows no signs of his condition and he travels the world lecturing about autism and the Son-Rise Program and is the author of the book *Autism Breakthrough: The Groundbreaking Method that Has Helped Families All Over the World.*[2] Ironically, all these years later, I can say that the little boy that I once saw depicted in that movie when I was 13 years old, the little boy at the center of a movie that changed my life, has been my dear friend and colleague for the last 30 years.

From that point onwards, working with children on the autism spectrum became my dream, my focus, and one of the great passions of my life. Throughout my teenage years, I would spend my summer holidays and spare time working in play schemes and after-school programs where I might encounter special children, and most importantly children with autism. One summer, to my great delight, I met my first child with autism; I was 15 and she was 14. She wore a helmet because she would bang her head, and was at least a foot taller than me due to the specially designed high-heeled shoes she wore to accommodate her toe walking. I was assigned to her for the day, and within seconds of our meeting she got me in a headlock and started walking, dragging me along. She walked straight out of the school building and headed for the white line in the soccer field. The only knowledge I had about autism and how to be with a child with autism was the movie I had watched. It had left me with two ideas: join the child in their own

---

1   Special note: Joining is a technique that is used to help and connect with our children when they are engaging in their repetitive behaviors/stims/isms. Please go to www.autismtreatment.com if you would like to know more about it. Or read Chapter 2 of my book, *The Autism Language Launcher*.

2   Kaufman, R.F. (2014) *Autism Breakthrough: The Groundbreaking Method that Has Helped Families All Over the World.* New York, NY: St Martin's Press.

world, and love and accept what they want, which in this case was to walk around the soccer field. So I concentrated as much as I could on enjoying the white line and the walking, and felt good that at least she wanted me with her. She was assigned to me for the rest of the summer, because when she was with me she never banged her head. This was my very first sign of the healing power of joining. We walked, laughed and played, and had the best time together. She was my first real-life encounter with autism, and I was hooked.

My second encounter was with a child of a family friend. He was three years old when I met him and was such a sweetheart. He loved to run back and forth from one wall to the other and turn light switches on and off. Again, when I was with him I focused on joining him in his activities and loving and enjoying being with him. I noticed how he would look at me and smile when I ran with him and I was touched by the loveliness of his personality. Seeing glimpses of his personality shine forth as I joined him consolidated the idea that there was a complete person inside this silent boy, and I wanted to find a way to reach him and help him communicate to the world. This only solidified my belief that joining a child in their activities was an incredible way to connect with them.

I went on to college to study music and education at Surrey University. I chose music because it was a subject I was good at and I had the idea that I might become a music therapist. The more I learned about music therapy the more I realized it was not the therapy for me. I think it is a wonderful therapy that does great work with children with autism, but for me it was too restricted; I wanted to work in a more varied way. I was still itching to work directly one-on-one with children with autism in a therapeutic way, and was discouraged with how long it would take until I was allowed to do that. I was told that in order to work directly with children one-on-one I would have to do more educational work and I did not want to wait—I wanted to work straight away.

On leaving university, instead of going for further academic studies, I went to work for Dr. Rachel Pinney, the author of *Bobby: Breakthrough of an Autistic Child* and *Creative Listening* and the founder of Children's Hours in North London. She worked with a variety of children, some of whom were emotionally disturbed, and a number who had autism. She truly was a genius with children; they loved her, and she had an incredible ability to connect deeply with them. Like most geniuses, she had a colorful character and loved to push people's buttons. She was 80 when I met her, and my initial interview took place while she was taking a bath. Having asked me a few questions about myself, she let me know that I had passed the test. "What test?" I asked. She then informed me that she liked to see how people reacted to different situations. The fact that I was not fazed by her being in the bath led her to believe that I would not be judgmental toward the children I would be working with.

Although she was 80 and walked with the help of crutches, she had a lively mind and soul. As part of my training with her I would accompany her on the different lectures she gave in her surrounding community. I would carry suitcases of books around for her. Amazingly, she carried around the book *Son-Rise* by Barry Neil Kaufman, which was the very story I had watched on television when I was 13! She trained me herself to work one-on-one with the children, and I spent every day working directly with children with autism. I was in heaven. I was struck by the intelligence and love each child showed me on a daily basis. It was here that I met a family who were going to the United States to participate in a special program for their daughter with autism. Although I had no idea what the program was, I jumped at the opportunity to have this adventure and learn another form of treatment for autism.

It was not until the second day of the program in America, when they showed us the NBC movie *Son-Rise: A Miracle of Love*, that I realized that this center was run by the family I had watched in the movie, which had inspired me to work with children with autism in the first place. Wow! That was a very awe-inspiring moment for me. I had come full circle, and it was as if in some way I had come home. I knew that I had found the methodology that I wanted to train and work in. Until that point, I had never encountered two particular traits found within this methodology. First, the staff were so sincere in their love and delight of the little girl I had come with that you could see it and feel it in everything they did. Second, they were also so powerful and effective in asking her to change and grow. They asked her to look at them, to use the spoken word, to dress herself. They helped her to grow so much during that week, and all within the context of truly enjoying and loving her.

I carried on my work with Dr. Rachel Pinney and then, instead of pursuing further study, I returned to the Autism Treatment Center of America to begin my formal Son-Rise Program training. I trained intensively for five years to become a Son-Rise Program child facilitator and Son-Rise Program teacher. This is about the same amount of time and energy it would take to get a PhD. My training was extremely hands-on. It is an in-depth training and has a strong emphasis on attitude. I worked directly with children and adults on the autism spectrum and got direct feedback from the senior staff. We were video-taped and then our time with each child analyzed, sometimes frame-by-frame or second-by-second. I also worked directly with parents and other family members, training them on how to work with their children, and received feedback on this. If we were to teach a principle or technique, we would be observed and then our explanations and sharing would be reviewed in detail by our trainers in order to help us to be the most effective communicators possible. We spent hundreds of hours exploring our own thoughts and feelings so that we could truly approach each child and each adult with an open, caring and accepting heart.

One thing the Son-Rise Program recognizes is that each child with autism can be so different, motivated by different things, and have varying degrees of complex challenges. I needed to be able to recognize these challenges, to connect with and help these children and families from the very moment of meeting them. Then I had to be able to articulate what I knew and teach it to many families so that they could work in this way with their own children. This took a lot of time and focus on my part and experience of different children and families to acquire it.

I have now worked with the Son-Rise Program at the Autism Treatment Center of America for over 30 years and feel so blessed to have supported so many children and their families, as well as trained over 40 Son-Rise Program professionals.

I have spent thousands and thousands of hours working one-on-one with the most lovely, silly, funny, determined and hard-working children and adults. I have never worked with a child who did not want to learn, who did not try their very best. I feel so grateful to have had so much time with each and every one of these children, for they have taught me what it means to open my heart, to listen and have the daring to try even the things that seem impossible at first. I have been talked to for hours on end about numerous different subjects from the magnificence of washing machines to the statistics of earthquakes, and I have joined thousands of unique and wonderful different "isms" ("isms" are what we in the Son-Rise Program call a child's repetitious behavior or "stims"), and motivations. I have thought up, created and then played thousands of games based on what our children love the most and am so happy to share some with you here.

Although I can never say that I have stopped learning and am sure that I will encounter many more wonderfully different situations, I can say that I have experienced many that you encounter today with your children. Although your child is unique, I am sure that I have worked with a child who has displayed some of the same behaviors, motivations, nature or challenges as yours. One of the great parts of my education and training is the depth and breadth of hands-on experience that I have to share with you. I know of no other training that exceeds this. I feel that I can say with confidence from my own heart that although I have never met your child or children, I know that I would love them. Their uniqueness and loveliness would not be lost on me, no matter what their behaviors are.

I am now in private practice, teaching parents – both individually and in groups – how to create the games and interactions I am going to describe to you in this book, as well as those in my previous books. I do this either via Zoom, by going to their houses, or in live interactive online group programs. Together with Raun K. Kaufman I am the co-creator of the Autism Crisis Turnaround Protocol and I run online programs for families, schools and group homes who are facing crisis situations with their loved ones on the spectrum.

I have worked with families from Thailand, Singapore, Africa, Malaysia, China, France, Poland, Russia, Slovakia, Argentina and Brazil, to name a few, and I frequently travel with our staff to Europe, Asia and North America to present the Son-Rise Program. It has been such a wonderful journey and I feel so blessed to have met and worked with so many amazing families and their children.

Among the most common questions parents ask me are, "What games can I play with my child/adult? What type of activities will motivate my child? "How can I encourage my child to play with me?" In answer to those questions, it is with great sincerity that I offer you this book.

Kate

PART 1

THE HOW TO

THE HOW TO

CHAPTER 1

The Seven Magic Ingredients

This book is filled with game ideas and creative activities, designed specifically for your child or adult on the spectrum and engineered to maximize connection and increase spontaneous social interaction. By social interaction, I mean eye contact, nonverbal communication, verbal communication, flexibility, facial expression, gestures, turn-taking and all the components of social exchanges.

The first part of this book talks about a mindset and techniques to adopt while engaging in the games and activities. These are the seven "Magic Ingredients." It is these that will greatly increase your effectiveness in inspiring your child or adult to want to play these games with you. They will help you play the games in a way that fosters the type of connection you are looking for and enhances social skills, ensuring that participation is fun, easy and non-pushy for you and the child or adult you care for. The second part of the book is packed with fun games, ideas and activities that are based around the motivations of your child or adult. You can do them exactly as they are described or adapt them to fit you both. (Don't worry; I will show you how to adapt them.)

This approach is based entirely on my experience of playing with more than 1500 magnificent children and adults on the spectrum, ranging in age from 18 months to 56 years old. Over the past 30 years, I have put in well over 15,000 hours of one-to-one play with these amazing souls, using the Son-Rise Program. Everything I say in this book comes from first-hand experience. It works! And, most importantly, it is down to earth and completely doable by you. Yes, you who are reading this book. You can significantly help your child or adult grow their social interaction yourself, no matter what your background or your education. You can do all these games and activities yourself in your own home. This book is also a great resource for all you amazing professionals, whether you are a speech therapist, an occupational therapist or a special needs teacher. You can use these concepts and activities in your classroom and therapy rooms.

Excited to begin? Me too! Let's get right down to it. Here come the Seven Magic Ingredients for game playing or activity-building with your child or adult on the spectrum.

Magic Ingredient 1: The magic of you! Become an integral part of the game or activity itself

THIS CONCEPT IN A NUTSHELL

Social interaction is not just about playing games or achieving skills, it is about interacting with people. If we want to help our children and adults socially interact, we must become a major part of the game or activity. We must think up and create games that put us in the center, or part of the action. This effortlessly creates "natural" opportunities for spontaneous eye contact, verbal communication and conversation, facial expressions, nonverbal gestures, flexibility, turn-taking and more, all through pure fun play.

How do we become an integral part of the game?

1. BECOME THEIR FAVORITE OBJECT!

Yes! You! A living breathing version of their favorite object—their motivation. I am picturing you becoming your child or adult's favorite motivation right now. It's going to be different and fun. That's what you were looking for when you picked up this book: different ideas that are tailored to, and work for, your loved one on the spectrum. If your child or adult likes vacuum cleaners, you become a human vacuum cleaner. If they like cars, become a human car. If they like prime numbers, become a human prime number. If they like dangling ribbons, become a human dangling ribbon. You may be thinking, "Interesting idea, but my child likes washing machines, talks about them all the time, how do I become that?" Well, don't worry, at the beginning of each section based on a special motivation there is a section called "Be it" which has three different ideas on how to do exactly that. Here's a sneak peek right now on how to become a human washing machine, taken from the Household Appliances section of games and activities in Part 2 of the book:

VERSION 1

- Get a giant box (see the "Materials" section in Chapter 3 to know how to get your hands on one of these).
- Open the top and the bottom so it becomes a tunnel and cut a round hole in the middle of each of the sides so that your arms can fit through it.
- Draw a few control buttons on the box—On/Off buttons, a dial for the different kinds of cycles (extra spin, delicate spin, economy wash and so on—just use the ones that are on your own washing machine).
- Cut a big circular flap in the front of the box so that it can be a door that will open and close.
- Climb inside it and put your arms through the holes in the side, and away you go! You are a human washing machine!

VERSION 2

- Get two big plastic bags or bin liners.
- Attach them to your chest and back (safety pins or masking tape work well for this). The bags are for you to load the clothes into.
- With clear sticky tape, stick an On/Off button to your shirt, just above the bags.
- Stick on a dial that shows different kinds of cycles—again just use the ones that are on your own washing machine.

VERSION 3

- Get a poster board and draw a big square washing machine shape on the front with the words "washing machine."
- Draw the On/Off button and a dial with the different kinds of cycles.
- Attach a plastic bag to the back of the poster board (for the clothes to go into).
- Get some string and attach a loop to the top of the poster board so that it can go over your head.

Abracadabra! You have three different ways to become a human washing machine. Now your child has reason to look at you, talk to you, interact and engage with you—because you are the motivation and the game itself.

Get the idea? Go ahead and read all the sections of "Be it," even if some of them are about motivations your child or adult is not currently interested in. It will give you more ideas on how to become whatever it is your child or adult is most interested in, and help you come up with creative ideas for particular motivations that may not be mentioned in this book.

2. BECOME GREAT AT A SUPPORTING ROLE

You are not always going to get the starring role in the game, but you can play the smaller supporting roles with great passion. This is often the case if the activity is making or building things together. Your adult is giving you a green light (see Magic Ingredient 7) and wants you in the game, but your role in the game is small, maybe even tiny. That is okay. In fact, feel super great about it. If you were an out-of-work actor and got a job as a walk-on speaking guest on a popular sitcom, you would be over the moon. It would be a breakthrough into the industry. Consider this the same; it is the breakthrough you are wanting—small with a chance to grow into bigger things. Your loved one is interacting with you. Every bit counts. Even if it is only for a second or two, that matters. Over time, seconds build up into minutes and then into hours and days.

Here's an example of a supporting role. I played with a delightful nine-year-old called Sammy who loved to draw cartoons. When he drew the cartoons, he would look and talk to me—he was in a green light. However, he made it clear that I could not suggest ideas for the cartoons or draw cartoons myself. My role was to be the audience and get him different colored markers when he asked. This was more than okay with me, and I was super excited that we were interacting in this way. While accepting my role "as it is," I began thinking up ways to make it as "big" as I could. When he asked me to get him a marker, I would hop up and dance to the marker box. Or do a funny walk. Or deliver the marker on a plate, or in the back of a toy truck. These little things inspired more spontaneous laughter, and eye contact. I invited some of the soft toy animals to be part of the audience, and we had some sideline conversations between us about which cartoon we liked the most. Every now and then Sammy would add in a comment.

The idea is to accept the role as it is and build it within the limits that are given. I did not try to be anything else but the audience and the marker getter. That built trust and allowed for more interaction within my role.

Build your role by adding a little flare—by singing, dancing, adding sound effects, using humor, introducing puppets, figurines or soft toy animal friends, and dressing up.

Adding to your supporting role with flare does not mean you drag it out, let it become difficult or take too long. You want to do it in a way that does not overshadow what your child or adult wants. Stay within the limits of your role so your child or adult does not decide to cancel your role or edit you out.

3. BECOME SUPER VALUABLE

Do something that your child or adult can't do that they will want you to do again. For example:

- Bounce them higher than they can by themselves.
- Dangle or shake the piece of string they like looking at from a great height.
- Throw lots of little ping pong balls up in the air so that they can watch them fall.
- Give your child a piggyback or ride that they like so much.

- Sing the song they love.
- Share super-fun facts about their favorite subject they love to talk about, which they might not know right now.
- Draw their favorite characters doing funny things.
- Make really cool sound effects.
- Read the book in a silly, funny voice.
- Give deep pressure to their feet, head or hands.
- Blow bubbles for them.

If we have something in the game that they want us to do again, then we will have created a good reason for them to want to look at us, or talk to us, or physically participate with us. We are motivating them to interact with us when they want the activity again, not just the toy itself. This way they are learning and growing their social interactive skills as part of the play, not by rote, or force or to get something unrelated, like food or computer time.

4. BECOME SUPER USEFUL

Actively look for ways to be super useful in the game. For example:

- If they drop something, pick it up for them.
- If they want you to say something in a particular way, say it in the way they like.
- When they ask for something verbally or nonverbally, get it for them immediately.
- If they want you to stop doing something, stop doing it immediately.
- Offer to carry things for them.
- Offer to build the tower for them, read the book, turn the page, adjust their pillow, fan them if they are hot.
- Offer a sweater if they are cold.
- Take their socks off for them.
- If they are looking for something, keep trying to help them find it. Don't give up, even if you do not know what it is.

Think of yourself as the most amazing personal genie in a bottle. Their wish is your command, but instead of having only three wishes, there is an unending supply.

This idea is the direct opposite to the over-used "play dumb" technique talked about a lot in the autism community. The "play dumb" technique is designed to get our children or adults on the spectrum to do something for themselves. This technique has two problems:

1. What we are wanting to do is not encourage our children and adults to do things for themselves; we want to encourage them to interact and be part of a team.
2. Our child or adult might do what we wanted them to do, but they are left with the feeling that we are difficult. Who wants to interact with someone who is difficult? Who wants to play with someone who plays dumb when we need their help?

We want to be the opposite of difficult. We want to be the most super-helpful, super-friendly playmate. That will encourage them to want to stay interacting with us just a few minutes longer, *and that is where the most important growth lies* (see Magic Ingredient 4).

5. BECOME GREAT AT SEEING THEIR FAVORITE PART OF THE GAME

Allow yourself time to really observe your child or adult and see what it is they truly like the most about the game. It might not be the obvious part of the game. For instance, let's say your child loves all kinds of different weather. You have created a game where you made fake snow by rolling up pieces of tissue. You are throwing the fake snowflakes in the air, and they are falling on your child. There are many aspects of this game that your child could like:

- Watching the snow in the air as it falls to the ground.
- Feeling the snow as it falls on their head, face or arms.
- Enjoying it falling on their hand but not their face (or vice versa).
- Feeling the anticipation of you pausing before you throw the tissue snow.
- Hearing you say, "Here comes the snowstorm" in your weather forecaster voice.
- Watching exactly where the snow lands in the room.
- Running excitedly away from the snow so that it doesn't fall on them.

- Getting to pick up all the tissue snowflakes at the end and give them to you while they count them.

Observe when your child or adult has the most expression of smiles or laughs, or where they are looking and what they are paying the most attention to. That is probably what they like about the game the most. Then make sure you do more of that. Spend more time on that, by adding fun variations to that part of the game. This will give them more reason to stay in the game and will increase the opportunities for spontaneous social interaction with you.

One young girl I worked with loved imagination games about traveling, or going to a birthday party, or a restaurant. On first glance you would assume that the big part of the game would be the birthday party itself, or what happens once you get to the travel destination. But no, her most important and fun part of the game was getting ready for these events. It was all about the preparation. If we planned to travel to France, we actually never even got to the airport. It was all about packing for the trip, not going on the trip. Once I saw that, then I knew which part of the game to focus on and add more fun to. Knowing this, I could help her stay in the game longer. She spontaneously looked and talked to me within the game, because I was focusing on the part that she truly liked, and not trying to get her to move on to the destination. I became the best party-planner and suitcase-packer and list-maker there was! Knowing this also informed any other games I initiated and created for her. I knew to put a planning aspect into them.

6. DON'T USE TOYS OR GADGETS THAT COMPETE WITH YOUR AMAZINGNESS

Here I am referring to electronic toys, such as:

- books that talk
- battery operated toys such as:
  - radio control vehicles and airplanes
  - toys that have flashing lights and beep or have sound effects
  - baby dolls and soft animals that speak
- electronic music
- all screens.

All these items can do things that you cannot. I can't sing like Beyoncé (although I do try). I can't propel my arms as fast as the remote-control helicopter. Or make my head flash blue or red like the siren on their electronic ambulance or police car. When toys like these are around, they pose competition to you becoming the center or part of the game itself.

So many of today's toys are designed with the idea to entertain children for solo play so that parents can have some time to themselves. This is not what we are shooting for in this book. Our children are great at solo play—that's why you are reading this book to encourage social interaction.

Magic Ingredient 2: The magic of using your child or adult's motivation in the game

THIS CONCEPT IN A NUTSHELL

Motivation is the key to everything. We work harder, learn quicker, and engage more when we are really interested and enjoying what we are doing. When we are motivated, our brain secretes neurotransmitters, such as BDNF (brain-derived neurotrophic factor), that enhance the connectivity between our neurons, thus improving learning capability, attention spans and memory. Put your child or adult's unique interests and motivations at the center of the game. This will heighten the possibility of them participating in the game. It will foster positive associations with social interaction. The more positive associations they have with social interaction, the more likely they will spontaneously start to seek it out and grow in this area of their development.

Put your child's motivation at the center of the game

Putting our child or adult's motivation at the center of the game is different from using their motivations as a reward for a job well done. Raun K. Kaufman called this "the reward principle" in his book *Autism*

Breakthrough (p.54). The reward principle is when we give our child or adult something that they love as a reward for a task completed; for example, once they have written their name, they get a favorite sweet, or if they catch a ball five times or answer some questions, then they get to play with their favorite toy. Now to be clear, the reason most professionals and teachers use this is because it does get our children and adults on the spectrum to do things. That's pretty awesome, there's no denying that. However, and Kaufman goes on to explain this further in his book, the reward principle has a couple of problematic side effects:

- It does not help us like the activity we are doing to get the reward. For example, I will pretty much do anything if you offer me a free massage or a night of tango dancing. I will happily scrub the floor and edit someone's work assignment if I know I am going to get that lovely reward at the end of it. But it won't do anything to change my enjoyment levels or desire levels about scrubbing the floor. This is where the problem lies. We are not wanting our children or adults on the spectrum to just tolerate social interaction and get through in order to get something else. We want them to want to socially interact, for the pure fun of it. The reward system promotes the opposite. It teaches that we have to do hard, unfun stuff to get to the good stuff. See how that is completely the wrong way around?
- It also begs the questions, what happens when we do not have the reward?

I am encouraging you to ditch this outdated model and do something entirely different. Have the activity and game you are presenting centered around what your child loves the most. If your child loves bubbles, then let's create games all about bubbles. If your adult likes numbers, then let's put numbers at the very center of the game. Your child or adult is more likely to look at you if you are talking about numbers or bubbles. They are more likely to want to participate and take turns and interact if the game is centered around what they already enjoy and like.

I am more likely to hang out with people who have similar interests to me. I socially interact with people who like what I like, who are interested in what I am interested in. I would be more drawn to someone who is reading a book on tango that I am to a person who is reading a book about Ancient Roman history. That is human nature; we bond and interact with people who have similar interests. When I look around the world I can see people who reflect the same interests as me. For those of you who like soccer, you can easily find someone who is thrilled to talk about soccer with you and go to matches. The same if you like musicals, ballet or shopping.

Children and adults on the spectrum don't usually see their interests reflected in the world around them. They have a different way of looking at and experiencing the world. They see and interact with toys and objects differently. I have so much experience with children and adults staring at the light, a spinning fan, or dust particles sparkling in the air. Listening to joyous fascinating facts about vacuum cleaners, toilets, weather patterns, World War II bomber planes, subway maps and road signs. Through my work with our amazing children and adults on the spectrum, I have come to see the magnificence of studying the details of the world from an alternative angle, seeing beauty in a light switch or piece of string dangling before my eyes. In order to bring our children and adults close to us and inspire them to want to interact with people, we must embrace what it is they are interested in, not try to get them to be interested in what we think they should be interested in.

Their interests that are different are often labeled as obsessions. As soon as it is branded that way, the whole focus becomes moving them away from it. Simply put, this alienates them from social interaction, does not work and creates many control battles. We learn when we are motivated.

I worked with Gabriella, a beautiful young seven-year-old on the spectrum, and her family. Gabriella was (like me) in love with food. She loved eating all day and looking at pictures of food. At that time, food was her only motivation. She centered nearly all her attention and focus around the topic of food. Her parents were constantly trying to pull her away from the subject of food and into other "more productive" subjects like math and writing, and show her more of what the world had to offer. They believed that her "obsession" with food was getting in the way of her learning and interacting. That is exactly why they were consulting with me. They wanted to know how to get her to stop being so focused on food. But from my perspective, the very thing that was stopping her from learning and interacting was the fact that the very well-intentioned people around her were trying to stop her from doing what she loved. As you are probably already guessing, we switched this around and put her motivation with food at the center of every activity and game we presented her with. It worked like—as the title of this chapter suggests—magic! Over the next two years she learned to speak through naming different foods. She learned math by cooking her favorite foods and measuring out different ingredients. She learned to be flexible and spontaneous by coming up with different recipes. She learned about the different cultures of the world by studying their foods. She even learned French and Italian!

So, how do you know what your child or adult's motivations are? It's easy; just look at:

- what they spend most time doing
- what toys they are drawn towards
- what they like to talk about
- what they like to read about.

Exercise

- Write down the top three things your child or adult likes to do when they are alone.
- Write down the top three things they like to do that include you in some way.

Already you have six possible motivations. If you are still not sure, browse through the different motivation sections of this book, and this may help you find some.

Also, at the back of this book is a motivation-finding worksheet you can do to get an even clearer idea of what motivates your child or adult.

Magic Ingredient 3: The magic of fun

THIS CONCEPT IN A NUTSHELL
Fun is a universal language. It is spoken by all cultures, all ages, all abilities. Fun is the reason your child or adult will stay

involved in the game and keep coming back for more. It is the glue, the spark, the heartbeat of these games and strategies. Fun is one of the core reasons we socially interact with another person. We like it; it is enjoyable. If you only took one ingredient and put it into your game, let it be this one. Fun is the name of the game!

Fun. Do you remember fun? Can you think of the last time you did something with your loved one on the spectrum that was just for fun—without an agenda for learning or changing or stopping or growing? And if so, can you remember not feeling guilty about it afterwards?

Getting a diagnosis for your amazing child or adult will have been a shock, and then, perhaps unsupported, you have to find a way through the onslaught of emotions and fear that can ensue. Then you search through the many, often contradictory, therapies and biomedical "remedies" out there. Understandably, fun can take a back seat in the face of this bombardment. I am here to encourage you to let your sense of fun out again; to give you permission to play in a way that is not only fun for your child or adult, but also fun for you; to throw out all the perceived rights and wrongs and the appropriate and inappropriate way of doing things. Because, fun does not have:

- shoulds
- have tos
- musts
- wrong ways
- right ways
- inappropriate play
- appropriate play

- drills
- regimens
- rules
- judgments
- expectations
- pressure.

Fun has:

- laughter
- smiles
- giggles
- facial expressions
- silly faces

- cuddles
- humor
- mistakes
- jokes
- silliness

- nonsense words and actions
- bodily sound effects
- excitement
- sincerity
- heart
- love
- dancing
- self-expression
- drama
- spontaneity
- anticipation
- delight
- wonder
- experimentation
- flexibility.

When we are having fun, enjoying ourselves, laughing, delighting, we often say, "Ah, that felt good!" or, "I needed that." Or, "Ah, that was good for my soul." After fun, we feel energized and full, not tired and drained. We then immediately want more of that in our lives, or more of that person in our lives. Do you or your child or adult ever say or feel that when they finish a therapy session? My guess is probably not. But that is what I am aiming for. That is what I want our children or adults to feel when they play with you or any other person. That is what they experience when their parents or loved ones start running the Son-Rise Program for them. I have had children not want the session to end, call me up on the phone to ask me to come over and do a session with them. During the 2020 pandemic lockdown, a bright, nonverbal six-year-old on the spectrum would dress smartly and wait by the computer so that he could see and play with me when I was helping his parents implement the Son-Rise Program. All they had to say was they were going to have a call with me, and he would go and wait by the computer. This was a child who was hyperactive and had a great challenge waiting for anything. There he was, practicing that skill all by himself because he wanted to have fun with me. Learning happens effortlessly when we are having fun. In contrast, unfortunately, they said he would run and hide when the speech therapist called. His parents believed I had some kind of magic—like Mary Poppins—but the magic I had was fun. I liked what he liked and exercised no judgment.

When families have visited the Autism Treatment Center of America to spend a week doing the Son-Rise Intensive Program, parents have told me that years later, as much as 10–15 years later, they were still talking about their time there, remembering each child facilitator and the fun they had with them, remembering all the games they played. One child was in the back of his mom's car (about three years after the program) when he said, "Remember when you took me to that place in the woods where Brandi and Becky played with me?" She said, "Yes." He replied, "That is where I felt the most loved and had the most fun." That is what we want our loved ones to be saying about their therapy sessions. That is what will inspire them to come back for more. That is what they are going to associate with interacting with you. Fun and warmth and love. That is a learning environment where social interaction can flourish.

How do I have fun?

I know this question may sound silly to some of you. You who are thinking as you read this, "Yay! I've got this! I know how to have fun. At last, I have permission to ditch the rules. Yahoo! Bring it on." I say to you—go for it, you fun master! Here, I am speaking directly to those of you who feel daunted by this ingredient, who may be thinking, "I'm not sure I know how to have fun." No worries, I've got you. This is something lots of parents have shared with me over the years. Below is a way of thinking about it and some steps that will start adding more fun to your every day, in a low-key, non-pressured way. It's worked for loads of parents and it can work for you if you open your mind to it and give it a chance.

THE DECK IS ALREADY STACKED IN YOUR FAVOR

That is the beauty of all the games in this book: they are already centered around what your child likes. (If your child's particular motivation is not represented in this book, see page 63 for how to use these ideas to modify the games to suit your child's particular interests.) Yes! Abracadabra! You are already halfway there. The content of the game will already be fun for your child. We don't have to worry about them; they will take care of their own fun. Let that take some of the pressure off you. Less pressure, more fun. With that taken care of, the only thing left is for you to focus on your own fun.

FOCUS ON HAVING FUN INSTEAD OF BEING FUN

Our children and adults know what they like, how they like to do it and are mostly not shy about expressing it. We, on the other hand, may have decided to focus more on being productive or serious about our life/career/family and have put "fun" on the back burner. So now let's get reacquainted with it.

It is easier to do something when we have beliefs that help and support us. Here are two beliefs that will, if you decide to adopt them, do just that:

- I believe I can find my "fun" again.
- Having fun will help my child or adult grow their social interaction.

With those two beliefs setting up shop in your brain, do the following three steps to get the fun factor simmering in your life.

REVIVE THE LOST FUN
Write a list of things you used to find fun, but don't find time to do any more. Remember, there is no right answer to this, this is your idea of fun. For example:

- Singing along to songs loudly in the car
- Listening to your kind of music
- Dancing
- Pranking your friends
- Learning new and unusual words
- Writing a poem
- Cooking some new and exciting recipe
- Watching stand-up comedy
- Reading fiction
- Crafting
- Making art
- Playing the guitar
- Doing the crossword
- Playing football/baseball
- Hanging out with the guys or your girlfriends.

Once written, read them out loud to yourself, so that you can hear them. You *do* know how to have fun, it's just that you allowed the responsibilities and emotions of being a special needs parent to over-shadow this part of yourself. It's time to bring them back in ways that are possible. By that I mean taking advantage of the micro moments throughout the day when you can. For example:

- Start singing in the car again—you don't need more time to do that.
- Start playing your own music in the car, or on your cell phone with headphones if need be. Play your own music as you are tidying up the day's mess once your child or adult is hopefully in bed.
- If you are cleaning your house, start doing it with a little dance in your step. No extra time needed to add that little bit of dancing fun into your step as you move around the house. One special needs mother friend of mine would dance at the supermarket to the music playing. Here, shopping time was her disco.
- If art is your fun thing, do micro drawings on your Post-It notes or shopping lists. Doodling is a form of art.
- Make up songs about what you are doing in the moment. For instance:
  "I am chopping the carrots!
  Oh yeah
  I can do it flare
  Oh yeah
  I chop them once, I chop them twice
  Chop, chop, chop
  I sure can slice."
- Play the guitar to your child or adult—a perfect addition to any game.
- Instead of reaching for a self-help guide or workbook, take ten minutes a week to watch a stand-up comedy routine.
- Get an audio fiction book and listen to it when you stack the dishwasher, do the ironing or drive to work.

This is not indulgent; this is helping your child or adult. Working your "fun" muscle will help you find more joy in your life which will make you more appealing for them to want to interact with you.

Maybe some of you are thinking, "I am just too tired to have fun." I would like to suggest that perhaps you are tired because there is not enough "fun" in your life. Fun gives us energy, not saps us of it. You may relate to the following scenario: *You have had a long hard day at work. Nothing went as it should and your boss gave you a hard time. You are tired, you want to go home and go to bed. But your friend calls you and wants to hang out for a while. Even though you feel too tired, you go anyway. You spend an hour with her and as you are walking to the car you realize that you have forgotten about your tiredness, the fun of the exchange having revived you.*

Perhaps not having fun is creating your tiredness more than the actions of special needs parenting.

SKIP
Skipping never fails to give a little lift to my spirits or add a little fun to my day. Yes, I am being totally serious; skipping is one of my shortcuts to lift me out of a serious mood and into the fun that is within my reach no matter what is happening in my life. Try it. It is impossible to skip and not smile. It seems to be inherently fun. Skip to the email box, to the school game, down the supermarket aisle. You can skip anywhere.

You can decide to have fun with anything
Fun is a state of mind. It does not lie in the activity itself. Fun starts inside our brains. It is a decision and a belief that something is fun. Realizing this gives us the power to create fun for ourselves instead of looking for it in an activity.

People like to do different things—they like snooker, swimming, skiing, cooking, reading, movies, eating out, tango dancing, tap dancing, disco dancing, ice skating, rugby, running, working out, knitting and so on. Everyone likes different activities. If it were the actual game or the activity that made it fun and exciting, then everybody would enjoy the same activities. Soccer might arguably be the most universal and widespread game enjoyed by people around the globe, but even that is not enjoyed by everyone. It is what the person actually decides to believe about the game that makes it fun and exciting for them. Maybe it was something the whole family played and it was the warmth of the whole family playing together that brought enjoyment to the game. Maybe it was the thrill of being celebrated for being good at a particular sport that added to the fun of the game. What we associate with the game can be more meaningful than the actual act of the game itself. In short, this means that we are in charge of how much fun we have at any given moment, with any activity.

This means that you can actively choose to have fun with any activity that your child or adult likes. Here are two steps to help you with this:

1. Look at each activity you present and find at least one component of it that you can decide will be fun. Maybe it is the sound effects you are going to make when you turn on the pretend vacuum cleaner. Maybe it is the fun of coloring in a rain cloud you are drawing. Then double your excitement and fun towards that aspect.
2. Once you genuinely and sincerely have fun with one component, then find another one, then another until you are having sincere fun with all the aspects of the game.

The more fun we are having with a game or activity the more sparkle we will bring to it. It will be our sense of enjoyment and fun that draws our children or adults to want to interact with us. Creating a game around what motivates our children or adults and then having sincere fun with it ourselves is the dynamite combination that stacks the decks in favor of fostering all aspects of social interaction.

Go forth and have fun!

Magic Ingredient 4: The magic of the unplanned

THIS CONCEPT IN A NUTSHELL

We want our play to be a two-way street. It is a collaboration with our very special child or adult on the spectrum, not a dictatorship. Let your game be malleable. Embrace their creative way of exploring it or changing it. Allow it to blossom into a new version. It is not the structure of the game itself that matters, but the interaction between you both. Their growth lies in the interaction not the precise execution of any game or activity. When we let go, everything becomes possible.

Expect the unexpected. You know the phrase from an old Yiddish proverb, "You make plans and God laughs?" Except just swop out the word "God" for the name of your child or adult. Yes, they are going to have other ideas. Your game is not going to go exactly as you planned it. If it does, yippee! But I can guarantee that that will be the exception not the norm. Accept that fact, and you will be able to see that every unexpected twist is just another great idea to add to the play.

Go with and weave back

I created a game for a child who loved sandcastles. I had two towels, a bottle of pretend sunscreen, dark glasses and a big beach ball. When he saw me with the towels he ran over and shouted with glee, "Wow! It's a magic carpet." He took the towels, laid them on the floor and jumped on them saying, "Abracadabra!"

If I had been rigid and too attached to the game I would have probably said, "No, it's a beach towel." Or, "But I wanted to play a beach game." Or "We can play magic carpets later," creating a right and a wrong way to play with the towel. This would have stopped the interaction and play. If our game becomes our agenda, our sense of fun and spontaneity flies right out the window. It will hamper us and close our eyes to other play opportunities staring us right in the face.

Instead, I was flexible and knew how to do what I call "go with and weave back." I celebrated his creative new twist and said, "Why yes, of course it is." I jumped on with him and we had fun flying around. (*This is the "go with" part.*) I said, "What do you see?" He said, "I see the moon." I said, "I see a beach in the distance." (*This is the "weave back" part.*) He said, "Where?" and I pointed ahead of us. He said, "Let's land there." We did. I got to add a little of my beach game before we hopped back on the magic carpet again and flew to a field full of flamingos. We hung out there and then went on to Mars, the bottom of the sea and Big Ben in London. Going with his game idea was way better than my idea alone.

Here's another example. I created a "surprise hat game." It was a big cardboard box with different hats in. The idea was to take turns hopping into the box, secretly choose a hat and pop out with the hat on. Instead, the lovely girl I was working with put the hats on her feet and used them to slide across the linoleum floor. This time I just did the first part of "go with and weave back" and did not weave back. Doing that was a double bonus: I got to interact with her in a wonderful hat-sliding game and still had another game I could use for a later session. A win–win situation. Insist on doing it your way and the interaction and fun can quickly disappear.

Grow interactive attention span

In both the above scenarios, the most important thing was that the interaction continued, not the specific structure of the game itself. Interactive attention span is really at the heart of what is challenging for our loved ones on the spectrum. Grow this and you are growing your child or adult's ability to socially interact with their peers. Interactive attention span is often mistaken for attention span. But interactive attention span is very different. Attention span is how long someone attends to an activity; for instance, how long your child can sit and do one thing, like do a puzzle, build blocks, draw, play with dolls or read a book. Children and adults on the spectrum are actually highly skilled when it comes to attention span. They can focus and attend to their stims (repetitious activities) for a very long time, and often have an attention span that is way above their typically developing peers. *Interactive* attention span is different; it is about the amount of time that they actually attend to another person. It is marked with exchanges between two people, such as:

- looks
- turns
- gestures
- sounds
- words
- smiles
- physical contact
- facial expression.

It does not matter what you are doing but how you are doing it. It could be coming up with a new vacuuming idea together, it could be reciting the times tables together, chasing one another, playing baseball or dressing up as superheroes. The important thing is that there is a clear exchange between the two of you. Grow these exchanges, lengthen your loved one's interactive attention span, and their ability to socially interact will skyrocket.

By playing in such a way that allows for the unplanned, you embrace your child or adult's unexpected responses and new directions—and you will be more likely to keep the interaction going. Becoming too rigid on how the game should be played will lead to less fun and less interaction, maybe even no interaction. That is why all the games and activities ideas in this book are designed to be open-ended, to allow for your child or adult's unique contributions to the game itself. They allow the game to take on a life of its own and help us leave our agendas for the office.

Trust that they are on their way to play your game

Although every person on the spectrum I have worked with is different and unique, they each have, to varying degrees, a super-sensitive sensory system, for which I will use Raun K. Kaufman's shorthand term "S4"[1] from now on. Because of their S4 they experience the world differently. They hear things differently, see things differently, experience smells and touch differently. This leads to them responding to events, games and activities in a radically different way from their typical peers. As a result, their effort to play, respond and attend looks different and can often be misinterpreted by us as being uninterested in the game presented.

For example, if they were playing a game with you and then started to stim, which is a red light (see Magic Ingredient 7), yes, it is time to stop playing the game because of their red light, but that does not mean that they are uninterested in continuing the game later, it just means that they are unable to continue at that moment because they need to regulate their S4. This may take five minutes, 30 seconds or two hours. Once regulated, they will show a green light signal and, if offered the same game again, they often will continue playing. We can misinterpret the red light as a statement of dislike of the game instead of a need to regulate their S4, and thus we don't reinitiate the same game and give them another chance to lengthen their interactive attention span.

Again, due to their S4 they have a heightened need for control. This, again, can be misinterpreted as being uninterested in the game when in fact they are actually just setting things up to help them be able to participate.

Milly was a great example of this. She was a 22-year-old not yet verbal adult on the spectrum. Whenever I presented a game to her she would immediately start pacing round the room five or so times, muttering to herself before she came and sat down beside me. Giving

---

1   Kaufman, *Live lecture*.

her time to respond was crucial, and if I had misinterpreted her need to pace as being uninterested in the game, I would have robbed her of the chance to play. Give your child or adult time to show interest.

Mohammed, an 11-year-old on the spectrum, would have to line up all his objects in a particular place before he started any game with me. He had three balls, a plastic fork and a wooden spoon. In order for him to play he had to place each object next to him, two on the left, three on the right. Each time we moved to a different part of the room he had to make sure each object came with him and took great care to reposition them. Allowing for this helped him stay in the game for longer. See these things as helping your child or adult stay in the game, not as a hindrance or a sign that they will not play.

Magic Ingredient 5: The magic of the pause

THIS CONCEPT IN A NUTSHELL

Our children and adults' processing speeds are different from ours. Often slower, much slower. Putting pauses into the game or activity gives our children and adults the opportunity to respond spontaneously. It gives them the chance to show us what they already know and what they can already do. It also gives them the chance to practice new skills, participating and taking their turn in the interaction.

During my early years playing with children and adults on the spectrum, I met Egor, a smart and funny nine-year-old. He taught me about really noticing the processing speed of the person I was working with. It took me four days of working with him to realize that he was responding to me five whole minutes after I had asked him to do something. It took me that long because of two limiting beliefs I held at that time. When he did not respond after a minute I had one of the following thoughts:

- He did not want to do it.
- He could not do it.

I then moved on to something else. Because my mind was on something else, it took a while to relate his delayed response to something I was doing five minutes ago. Once I got this, everything changed for me. First, this real-life experience helped me ditch the two beliefs I set out above that really stopped me from seeing Egor's responses. Second, I learned the importance of attentively listening and watching for processing speed. I think Egor was relieved that someone finally got that he was responding and could play the games, just at a much slower speed. His social skills and interaction skyrocketed when his parents and his support team added in pauses of five minutes so that he could participate.

Pauses are not just about processing speed; they are about turn-taking and interaction. To have a conversation you have to leave space for the other person to talk. To play a game you have to stop and let the other person have a go. Check in with yourself and ask yourself the question, am I leaving space for my child or adult to participate in the game? When we have a child or adult who has not spoken yet, or who does not always respond, we can easily fall into the trap of not allowing opportunities for them to do so. Adding more pauses will give your child or adult the opportunity to respond.

Pausing without prompting

This is an extra golden piece of magic to add to your ingredients. This does not mean that you can't ever prompt your child or adult to say a word or verbally request something very specific, like:

- Which one do you want?
- Turn the page.
- Come dance with me.
- Your turn to sing.
- Write down three wishes.
- Draw a kangaroo.
- Catch the bubble.

That is definitely something you are going to do a lot in the games and activities you play with them. However, I am going to suggest that you balance that with at least 50 percent of the time pausing with:

- no prompt (such as, "say banana")
- no request (such as, "pick up the blue wig")
- no nonverbal direction (pointing to something, or gesturing for them to come here, or hand over hand).

Over-prompting and over-directing our children or adults in exactly what to do next creates the robotic behaviors and mannerisms that the autistic community is falsely accused of. This robotic behavior is a by-product of over-prompting and over-requesting. The key to encouraging more natural and spontaneous response from our children and adults is to pause without agenda or direction.

A pause without a prompt looks like this:

- You stop doing whatever it is you were doing.
- You are totally silent.
- You look at your child or adult with an expectant, interested, friendly expression on your face. An expression meant to silently say, "I can't wait to see or hear what you want to contribute to this game or conversation."

When you allow pauses without prompts or direction, surprising things happen. I was playing with Sonya, an adorable four-year-old on the spectrum. I had created a game of sliding hats and wigs across the room. She seemed interested in watching them slide along the floor. After enjoying doing this for a few minutes, I paused without prompting her to do anything, giving her a chance to spontaneously contribute to the game. I thought she might ask me to slide them again, or hand me one to slide. Instead, she picked up a long blond wig, came over to me and said, "You are a Barbie." Ha-ha! Barbies were far from my thoughts at that time. If I had not given her that pause, I would never have known that Barbies were on her mind. We then proceeded to play, pretending to be Barbies, for the next 20 minutes. This unprompted pause allowed for this unplanned play to occur, which lengthened her attention span by 20 minutes, and produced a couple of four-word spontaneous sentences that were new for her. If we want our children to become spontaneous, we must leave unprompted pauses within the play.

How long to pause?

Experiment to find out how long it usually takes for your child or adult to respond. It can range from ten seconds to anything up to the five minutes that Egor needed. Ten seconds can seem like nothing when you say it, but time it, and most of you won't be waiting even ten seconds before moving on and responding for your child or adult.

Remember that children and adults on the spectrum change all the time. Check in every three weeks or so to see if their processing speed has changed. If you are regularly playing with your child or adult and adding in pauses, you will most likely see the rate decrease over time, simply because you have given them the opportunity to work this skill by adding in more pauses to your games and activities.

How much to pause?

I have yet to see someone over-pause. Think about it as a conversation. If you are in a conversation with a person who is speaking more than you, you don't have to add in pauses because the other person is already contributing a lot. If you are the main one talking, you must consciously add in more pauses to allow the other one to speak. Most professionals and parents I have worked with underutilize this magic ingredient.

When to pause?

- Just after you have asked your child or adult to do something.
- Just before you get to a point in the game that your child or adult is most excited about. This the sweet spot in the game or activity. It is when your child or adult is at their most motivated. Usually that would not be at the beginning or at the end, but mostly in the middle. For example, if you are playing a game where you are blowing bubbles, and your child or adult is really enjoying seeing the bubbles come out of the bubble wand, pause without a prompt just before you are about to blow. So you will already have the bubble wand up to your mouth and have taken in a deep breath, then you turn and look at your child or adult and pause. This gives them a chance to ask for the bubble at the height of their motivation for the game.
- Once a game has got going and is under way, pause and give

your child or adult the opportunity to contribute to it in some way.

- Pause in the middle of a story you are telling, at a crucial part in the story, just before you get to the main event. This is a cliff-hanger. Most TV series end an episode on a cliff-hanger to encourage the viewer to watch the next one. Here the pause gives the space to our children and adults to interact, and to get you to carry on the story, or participate in the conversation.

Magic Ingredient 6: The magic of celebration

THIS CONCEPT IN A NUTSHELL

Celebration makes everything better. It feels good to be acknowledged, loved and sincerely appreciated by the people in our lives. This is, in my opinion, one of the most powerful actions we can take to create a strong, thriving learning environment. Our children and adults on the spectrum will move towards and do what we celebrate. Simple. If you want your child or adult to keep doing something, celebrate it. The more you celebrate, the more likely they will continue to do it.

If I asked you if you celebrated your child or adult, I believe you probably would say yes, of course. And yes, you do. However, if you thought back to yesterday, how many times did you verbally celebrate them for interacting with you? For looking at you? For making a sound or saying a word? For coming over to you and sitting beside you? For leaning on you or giving you their toy or shirt or cup? Did you celebrate them when they got in the car when you asked them to? Or that they went to bed or sang a song, or gently put a hand on your shoulder? If there were a hundred possible moments to celebrate them in your day, how many of those moments did you celebrate? Ten? Three? Thirty? Be really honest with yourself. This is not a test of how great you are as a parent or a professional. You love your child or adult; you want the best for them. If you can be honest and really see that most likely there is room to grow in this area, you will be able to unleash one of the most powerful forces to help your child or adult play interactively with you. You move towards love and celebration.

When we celebrate our loved ones we show them the way to move forward. Each celebration is like a road sign that says, "keep moving this way, that's right, come this way." Our celebrations light the way towards what social interaction is.

We want our children and adults on the spectrum to feel the true warmth of socially interacting with another person. Enjoying another and being enjoyed is what makes an interaction wonderful and keeps us coming back for more.

What to celebrate
Celebrate the following:

- All interaction:
  - All eye contact
  - All sounds
  - All words
  - All physical contact
  - Every response to a request
  - Each time your child or adult gives you something
  - Each time they take something from you
  - Every time they take part in the game or activity.
- All effort. Effort may be the most important thing to celebrate. Socially interacting is challenging for our children and adults. They are not always going to get things right the first time round. If we can help them fall in love with trying and practicing, it will skyrocket their growth. All growth takes effort. Love that process and then everything becomes achievable. Celebrate all effort!

How to celebrate
Celebration is you feeling a sense of joy at something your child or adult does and then telling them that. Here are three things I want to highlight about celebrating:

1. **You cannot celebrate too much.** I am often asked the question, "Can you celebrate too much?" I think it is a testament to the

state of the Western world. We as a society are so focused on the next thing, we somehow feel lazy if we allow ourselves to savor what we already have. There is also the notion that we will make the child or adult bigheaded. I have never seen that happen as a result of the celebration, but what if it did? If you had a bigheaded, socially interactive child or adult, would you be complaining? So celebrate like there is no tomorrow, and if you think you are over-celebrating, celebrate some more. Celebrate every time your child or adult interacts with you, looks at you, makes a sound, holds your hand, gives you something. Yes, every time. Not just once, not just the first time, every time. This is one of the most powerful things we can do; let them know that they are loved, that you want them to interact with you, that it *is* a big deal. Allow yourself to savor them playing with you. *The more you do, the more likely they will savor being with you.*

2. **Be very specific.** Instead of saying, "Yay!" when they look at you, be specific about what you are saying "Yay!" about. Say, "I loved that you just looked into my eyes; you have the best eyes ever." Or, "I so love playing this game with you." "You threw that ball amazingly well." "You are the best drawer ever." "Wow, I love it when we tell each other stories." "Wow, you are just a great friend. I love it when you tell me about your day." "Thanks for letting me take a turn in the game." "Isn't it great that we get to play this game together!" "You were so funny when you pretended to be a dog—you rocked it!" "Thanks for getting that for me."

3. **Be sincere and vary your celebrations.** The magic of a celebration is that it comes from a deeply sincere place. Each time you celebrate, allow yourself to get in touch with how amazing it was that they just interacted with you. Interacting is hard for them, so it's a big deal when they do. Really allow yourself to feel that and express your delight in their interaction. And remember to vary your celebration. It can be easy to fall into a rut of saying the same thing each time. This can get monotonous for you and your child or adult. Change it up. Below are different ways you could celebrate:
   - Big and crazy

- Silly and goofy
- Cheerleader
- Sweet and sincere
- Whispering
- Singing
- With big gestures.

Magic Ingredient 7: The magic of timing

THIS CONCEPT IN A NUTSHELL

Our children and adults on the spectrum are giving us two types of signals throughout the day. A green-light signal that tells us they are ready to play and connect with us, and a red-light signal that tells us that they are overwhelmed and unable to connect and take in anything new at that moment. If you want to be successful at playing games interactively with them, only initiate the games and activities in this book at a green light and stop the game or activity at the red light.

When to initiate the games or activities in this book

Okay, now we have discussed all the different ways we can be in the game or activity that will greatly increase social interaction, connection and the likelihood of participation. It leaves one major question still to answer: When do I introduce these games? No one really ever addresses this: everyone focuses on the what to do, but not on *when* to do it. The when is just as, if not more, important than the what and the how to do the games and activities. You may say, "Well, can't I just initiate the games whenever I have some time?" Not if you have a child or adult on the spectrum.

Why? Because your child or adult oscillates between two very different brain states. In the Son-Rise Program we call these two brain states a green light and a red light. A red light is when their brain is overwhelmed. Their extremely sensitive sensory system is overloaded, and they are not able to take in new information or learn something new. Their brain is, so to speak, "closed for business."

At these times, they will need to go within and focus on self-regulation. A green light is when their brain is "open for business." It is a time when they are more regulated and thus are able to connect, play and learn new things.

Obviously, we only want to introduce games and activities when our children and adults' brains are ready and "open for business." Part of the challenge you may be having engaging your child or adult is that you are trying when they are in a red light and less able to engage. Let's say you are in the middle of the airport, you have been traveling for the last 24 hours, only had two hours of sleep, are trying to navigate a different language, while carrying three suitcases. Someone comes up to you and wants to teach you a new dance routine. Now, you like dancing and normally would love this invitation, but in this moment your brain has no room for it. You just do not have any brain power left to do it. I know that sounds really extreme, but it is similar to what our children and adults go through on a daily basis. They are constantly asked to grow and change and do things that are difficult for them in the middle of times when they are overwhelmed. Not fun. That's what they then associate with interacting with people. Let's change that by only introducing games when they are in a green light.

Don't worry; it is very easy to know when they are in a green light or a red light. Your child or adult on the spectrum is sending you signals; you just have not decoded them yet. I am going to give you the secret magic code. Finally, you will understand why sometimes they will play and engage with you and sometimes they will not. Here they are.

Knowing the signals
GREEN LIGHTS
Your child or adult is open to engaging and interacting with you and others when they are:

- not involved in a stim or repetitive activity
- looking at you
- verbally communicating with you
- responding to you when you speak to them
- flexible about what game or activity you are playing and how the game or activity is happening

- being physically affectionate with you
- showing an interest in what you are doing (e.g., they might be looking at the objects or toys you are moving around).

A highly verbal green-light signal:

- Your child or adult is pausing to let you speak.

Note: Your child or adult does not have to display all of these signals; just look for one or two of them.

RED LIGHTS
Your child or adult seems to be in their own world and not engaging with you or others when they are:

- involved in their stim or repetitious activity
- not looking at you
- not responding to you when you speak to them
- insisting that things go a particular way, and seeming inflexible, rigid and controlling
- saying "No" a lot or asking repetitious questions.

A highly verbal red-light signal:

- Your child or adult is speaking without leaving room for you to speak.

Now you know them, all you have to do is observe and look for these signals. Just observe them for five to ten seconds. Yes! It really is as easy as that.

Following their lead
The first step on your journey to becoming the best game and activity player with your loved one on the spectrum is to become super great at seeing their green and red lights. This may take a few days or a week to get skilled at. So do take some time to observe your child or adult for 30 minutes each day for a week. During that time, only focus on observing them for green- and red-light signals. As you observe the

lights, write down what they are. This will help you become really familiar with your child or adult's specific green and red lights. Giving yourself this time to observe and learn will also help you to understand how your child or adult can fluctuate between the two different brain states throughout the day. You will most likely find that no two observations are the same. Maybe one time your child or adult is in a red light for the whole 30 minutes. Another time they are in a green light the whole time. The next time you observe they interchange between red and green ten times. This is really important to understand as it will vary from day to day and session to session. But now you have a great tool to notice and follow your child or adult's signals.

For now, when you see that your child or adult has returned to a red light, stop the game. There is much more to learn about red lights and what to do to bond with your children or adults when they are in a red light, but as that is not the topic of this book, I will not go into that now. If you want to know where to find out more about that, go to the resources page at the back of this book for details.

As with partner dancing, such as tango or salsa, there is a leader who gets to create and decide what steps you are going to do, and a follower who gets to follow the leader's choice. In our case, it is our children and adults on the spectrum who lead. We follow by initiating games at the green light and stopping the game at the red light, then reinitiating the game at the next green light, stopping at the following red light and so on. We create a beautiful dance, guided by our loved child or adult.

This is going to feel so much better for you. It takes away the push and pressure to make the game work when it is clearly not working. Some of you may be thinking, well if I do that, I will not get to introduce these games very often. Yes, for some of you that may be true. But when you do, your child or adult will be in the position to actually take it in and engage with it, even if it is only for a few minutes or a moment. They will engage for longer as time goes on. The ironic thing is that even though you will be initiating less, your child or adult will more likely actually engage more. Both of you will get enjoyment from the experience. That will keep you and them coming back for more.

CHAPTER 2

Magical Thinking

I was training two students, Mary and Maya, to become professional Son-Rise Program child facilitators. They had both taken a video of themselves playing with the same child on the same day. The child was adorable Kojo, a four-year-old child on the spectrum. Kojo loved playing with his father's old ties. He had five of them. He would take them with him everywhere he went. He loved to roll them up and then unroll them and then roll them up again.

I watched Mary's video first. Kojo would give her really obvious long green lights (see Chapter 1, Magic Ingredient 7). He would look at her, come over to her and sit on her lap and touch her face. When this happened, Mary was wonderful in noticing and celebrating him but then she did not offer anything to him. She just sat there and looked at him. When I asked her why she did not present him with anything she said, "I just did not know what I could do with the ties. I mean a tie is a tie. I am not a very creative person."

I then watched Maya's video and Kojo was giving her the same obvious long green lights. Maya also celebrated in a big beautiful way, then she picked up a tie and spun it around her head like a lasso. As she did, she belly laughed. Then she got up and ran across the room dangling the tie so the bottom of it dragged across the floor. She kept running back and forth across the room with the tie following behind her. Kojo was watching her doing this and laughing with delight as the tie moved fast across the floor. Maya saw his delight and said, "Try and catch it." He got up and played a "Catch the Tie" game for the next three minutes or so. Three minutes of back-and-forth interacting was a long time for Kojo. When I asked Maya what she was thinking about the ties she said, "Oh, I believe anything can become anything. I am really creative like that."

Same child, same object, two different outcomes. What made the difference was what each of the students was thinking. One believed that she was creative, so she was. The other believed she wasn't and so fulfilled that prophecy and made herself stuck. Two different beliefs created two different outcomes.

Clearly, what we think and the beliefs we hold has its own kind of magic. It affects our actions, our gestures and our body-wide communication. This is then transmitted to the child or adult we are wanting to interact with and has a huge effect on their responsiveness. This is exciting, because although you are not in charge of how that child or adult responds to the games you present to them, you are in charge of what *you* think and feel.

Below are my top five beliefs to hold when you are creating and presenting these games and activities. I call them "Presto Chango" (that's "change-oh") beliefs, for two reasons:

- First, because it is hard to say "Presto Chango" without smiling, and, as this book is about playing, the sillier and the less serious we can be the better!
- Second, because if you do decide to adopt them, "Hey presto!" they will change everything about how you are with your child or adult on the spectrum.

"Presto Chango" Belief 1

"I am creative and can make anything fun!"

So many of us feel that we are not creative and not "fun" (whatever that means!). This belief sucks all the magic out of any activity before it has even begun. And, truly, it's just a belief—just an opinion or preconception that you have adopted. It is changeable. And, if you want all of the "magic" in this book to work, this belief has got to change.

Creativity is often conceived of as a rare and finite special talent of the few. Great musicians, artists, writers and performers (and maybe some renowned corporate CEOs?) possess this remarkable gift, and the rest of us merely watch in awe. This is not true—and rather silly. We all have a human brain, and that brain has a limitless capacity to generate thoughts and ideas. And, since you too have a human brain, then you have a bottomless wellspring of creativity to draw on...*if* you don't squelch it.

Give yourself a chance. What you have done or not done up to this point doesn't mean a thing. Don't let it hold you back. You're getting new information and ideas from this book. Your loved child or adult on the spectrum is always changing and growing (whether others see it or not). You are both in a different place now.

All change begins in your mind. That doesn't mean that "if you think it, it will happen." But it *does* mean that, in order for you to change your approach (and in order for your child or adult to then respond to that new approach), you have to *first* have a new thought or belief. That's the only way. And that's why you are going to make it happen, you superstar!

"Presto Chango" Belief 2

"My child or adult will find this interesting!"
Is it possible that your child or adult will *not* find the activity interesting? Of course! The title of this chapter isn't Magical Facts, after all. It's about how you are *thinking* and what you are *believing*. Why? Because this is what will determine how you approach your activity and how you interact with your child or adult. And *that* will have a massive effect on how they respond and engage.

Very, very often, people *begin* with the belief that their child or adult on the spectrum will just not be interested. Maybe their child or adult wasn't interested in the past. Maybe they have never tried this activity. Perhaps they have never seemed interested in *anything*.

Included in the "My child or adult will find this interesting!" belief is the following belief: "Just because my child or adult did not play it yesterday does not mean that my child or adult won't play it today." So, you're not going to trap them in the past. With magical thinking, you are going to wipe the slate clean and give your child or adult a chance to flourish in a new way. At the very beginning, you say to yourself, "They will love this!" That's your starting point! You're going to change the dynamic by changing your perspective—which will affect the tone of your voice, the expression on your face, your enthusiasm, your silliness, and your perseverance.

What happens if, even after adopting this belief 100 percent, your loved one doesn't seem interested? That leads to…

"Presto Chango" Belief 3

"I can have fun even if my child or adult does not respond in any clear way."

Hey! Guess what? You don't need your child or adult to respond in a particular way in order for *you* to have a blast! *You* are in charge of that! As strange as this might sound, you can use their seeming lack of response to *ramp up* your silliness, zaniness, energy and, yes, joyfulness! But you can only do this by taking on the belief that *you* bring the fun.

If you need a particular response from them in order to bring the fun (and enjoy yourself), then two problems arise. First, you will have times with your child or adult when you are not enjoying yourself (i.e., when they are not giving you a response that you deem "interested"). Second, they will pick up on this difference in your responses and it will create a dynamic where there is pressure on them to respond so that you are happy. And if there is one thing we all know, it's that if our children or adults on the spectrum feel a push, they will dig their heels in or move in the opposite direction.

Autism Abracadabra means making activities and games happen like magic—easily and with joy! So we have to bring the magic, not stamp it out!

"Presto Chango" Belief 4

"My attempt *is* the success!"

Remember that you don't want to push or pressure your child or adult by conditioning your good feeling and positive response on *their* response.

Actually, you can condition your good feeling on something you *can* control: your efforts! Your willingness to play with them! It's time to rejig what constitutes "success." No longer will it be defined according to what your child or adult does or does not do. Now, you are going to base it on your attempt. Your attempt *is* the success!

You may be wondering: but is it, though? The answer is an une-quivocal "Yes!" Why? Because, every time you attempt an activity or game, you are doing two very important things. Number one, you are expressing your love and caring to your child or adult. You think that doesn't matter? It matters more than anything else! Number two, each time you attempt an activity, you are laying the groundwork for something far bigger with respect to their development. You are showing them that it is safe, fun, pressure-free and exciting to interact with you (and, thus, other human beings). There is little that is more vital to their long-term growth. In his book *Autism Breakthrough*, Raun K. Kaufman describes it this way: "You are the ambassador of your world" (p.144). Everything you do communicates to your child or adult (whether this is your intention or not) what it is like to be part of our world. Is our world judgmental? Coercive? Disapproving? Stressful? Or is it non-judgmental? Pressure-free? Loving? Fun? Celebratory?

It is your presentation of the game (rather than whether or not your child or adult plays it) that determines what kind of ambassador you are.

"Presto Chango" Belief 5

"My child or adult's response is *not* a statement about my parenting, my skill, how interesting I am or how successful I was with my child or adult."

This belief is crucial! In order to make Autism Abracadabra happen, we need to decouple our children or adults' actions from our self-concep-tion. What your child or adult does or does not do means absolutely *nothing* about you! It says nothing about how well you did the activity, how good the activity was or how fun you are. And it *certainly* doesn't say anything about how good a parent you are!

You love and care for a child or adult on the autism spectrum! There are many, many reasons why your child or adult does the things that they do. They have an enormous amount of challenge to contend with. Making what your loved one does reflect on you will make you feel terrible, put pressure on them, and is just empirically not accurate when it comes to a child or adult on the spectrum.

Adopting this key belief can have wonderful and far-reaching consequences. It transforms your emotional well-being. It will make you better at introducing and playing the games in this book. It opens the door for your child or adult to interact with you because they want to, rather than to satisfy your self-esteem. And it creates a beautiful atmosphere for you and them to relate to each other!

So flip that switch and take on a new perspective! The power is in your hands!

Armed with these five "Presto Chango" Beliefs and the seven Magic Ingredients you are ready to go on to Chapter 3, which contains all the practical information you want to know about the games themselves.

Open Sesame: Starting, Stopping and Modifying the Games

Starting and stopping

When do you start the game or activity?

Introduce your game or activity only when the child or adult you want to interact with is in a green light (see Chapter 1, Magic Ingredient 7). This is really important. When they are in a green light, their brain is more available to be able to take in the game you are presenting. They will be more available to interact with you. That's it. It is really that simple. You introduce your game at a green light. For some of you this will be a complete turnaround on how you interact with your child, in that you will be looking to them and their signals to know when to introduce your game. It may mean that you can introduce your games and activities much more often than you had been doing before. Or, it may mean that you will be doing it less. Either way, if you decide to do this it will increase the attention and interaction your child or adult can devote to the game you are offering.

When do you stop playing the game or activity?

The stopping of the game is just as important as the starting. We do not want to "game" past our child or adult's red light (see Chapter 1, Magic Ingredient 7). Their red-light signals are telling us that their brain is in overload. Of course, that is not the time to be asking them to interact or play or connect with you. That is a time to let them regulate themselves with their stim. You don't have to worry about when to stop; they will show you by giving you a red-light signal.

A red-light signal is the sign to stop playing for now, not forever. Think of it like a pit stop, or a power nap, or a night's sleep. We all need them, and once we have them, we are refreshed, powered up and ready to play again. It is a sign of overload not an indication of disinterest or dislike of the game or activity. When you stop playing a sport or game because you are tired, it does not stop you from either continuing to like and enjoy the sport, or from wanting to play it again in the future. It can be the same for our children and adults on the spectrum. See their red light just as a break and try not to interpret it another way. Doing that will open up so many more opportunities for them to keep playing the game once they have regulated themselves. Once your child or adult gives you another green light, introduce the same game they had been enjoying or exploring just before they went into a red light. This gives them a real chance to continue what they had been enjoying before, helps them with their interactive attention span and communicates to them that they can take a break and continue when needed without the game or activity disappearing.

Another good time to stop a game is when it has finished. That's not as silly as it sounds. Some of the games and activities you introduce will have an obvious ending, and if that is the case check in with your child or adult to see if they are still in a green light and if they are, stop there and initiate a different game, or start the same game again. The idea is to keep interaction going for as long as they are in a green light and stop when they are in a red light. Yes, I am happy to say, it is as simple as that!

How do you start the game or activity?
MODEL IT FIRST
When you notice that your child or adult is giving you a green light, that is the signal that the time is ripe for the game playing to begin. Model the game first by playing it yourself. If you need a partner to model it fully, I am sure the stuffed animals and figurines would love to help you out. Play/model the game with all the fun you can muster. This is the selling part. It is important that your child or adult sees the game in action so that they know how fun it is going to be and why they should play it.

In this regard, your child or adult on the spectrum is just like us. We want to watch the movie trailer before we buy tickets for the movie. We want to see pictures of a house before we decide to take action and go to see it with the realtor. Our child or adult is more likely to do things that are difficult for them if they can see the fun they are going to have.

This is the part where you are doing all the play. You are not asking them to do anything. You are not challenging them; you are showing them and entertaining them with your game. This is where you can go crazy with your entertaining skills. For example, if your game is "Superhero Bowling," set up the bowling pins and knock them down three times yourself before you invite your child or adult to do it. As you are doing that, don't forget to have fun. Be silly and enthusiastic. This is your chance to sell the amazingness of the game. Really allow yourself to get into it. Cheer yourself if you knock the pins down. Do a little dance. Prepare yourself to throw the bowling pin in an elaborate and fun way. No one but your child or adult will be watching. Let yourself really get into it. You are a superhero bowling champion!

If it is a drawing game, such as, "Draw your child or adult's favorite book on the whiteboard," start drawing immediately. Draw the first page as you recite the story, then the second page and so forth. Not briefly but for at least one minute or more. Again, give it all you've got. With all your enthusiasm and excitement, show your fun! Why should your child or adult join you if you are not having fun? You want your game to be where the party is!

VERBALLY EXPLAIN THE GAME/ACTIVITY

Verbally explain your game as you are modeling it. For those of you whose child or adult is fully verbal, this makes complete sense. For those of you whose loved ones have yet to say a word or are not yet speaking in sentences, this may be a challenging idea. But just because they have yet to speak or speak very little does not mean that our children or adults don't understand what is being said to them. Their lack of speech or response can be mistaken for a lack of understanding, but this is not the case. It is my experience that they understand more than they are able to let us know. I explain this more in my previous two books. If this concept is new for you, please do read those chapters (see the Recommended Reading and Resources section at the end of the book for details). For now, take a leap of faith and verbally explain the game to your child or adult; you have nothing to lose by doing so, and everything to gain.

LOOK FOR ENJOYMENT SIGNALS

As you are introducing the game, look for any signals your child or adult is giving that may indicate what they like most about the game and do more of that part. Observe the following:

- Are they looking at one particular part of the game?
- Do they smile at a certain part?
- Do they laugh at a particular part?

Then do more of that part. Make that part bigger, longer or louder.

GIVE THEM A ROLE IN THE GAME/ACTIVITY

Although our children and adults can respond in many unique ways, there are three common ways they might respond when you model and entertain a game/activity at a green light:

1. **They will watch for a moment and then go back to a red light.** If this happens, you know what to do. You stop playing the game and think the "Presto Chango" Belief 4, "My attempt *is* the success!" (see Chapter 2).
2. **They spontaneously come and start playing the game with you.** If this happens, use Magic Ingredient 6, celebrate their participation and keep playing the game. As you play the game, don't forget to use Magic Ingredient 5 and pause to allow them to continue being spontaneous within the game.
3. **They keep watching you as you model the game, they might even smile and laugh at certain points, but they remain as an observer.** If this happens, invite them to participate by giving them a role in the game. In the games section, you can choose any of the suggestions from the "Things you could invite your child/adult to do." Or invite them to do something that is not on the list. The role I would suggest you invite first would be one of physical participation. Being given a physical role in the game can be easier for some of our children or adults and will

help them be more invested in the game. Physical participation could be them pretending to eat, picking up an object, throwing a ball, giving them your hand, getting inside a box, turning a page in a book, drawing, dancing and so on.

The games themselves

The games section is divided into motivation sections. I have included the most common subjects and things that our children and adults on the spectrum enjoy. There are sections for: letters, cell phones, household appliances, animals and insects, road signs, maps, traffic lights and subways, numbers, books, dangling things, vehicles, movies, cartoons and TV shows, weather and sensation/sensory seeking. Grouping the games in this way is designed to increase the possibility of interaction happening between you and your loved one on the spectrum. Magic Ingredient 1: "The magic of you! Become an integral part of the game or activity itself" (see Chapter 1) is already woven into the heart of every game. Every game is designed so that you have a starring or supporting role in the game itself, heightening the possibility for spontaneous eye contact, turn-taking, verbal communication, nonverbal communication, enjoyment, an exchange of smiles, laughter and facial expressions.

Magic Ingredient 2: "The magic of using your child or adult's motivation in the game" (see Chapter 1) is obviously also taken care of as these games are designed around our children and adults' particular motivations and interests. If your child or adult's unique motivation does not fit one of the categories that's okay, I've got you covered. The next part of this chapter shows you how to modify a game to make that game center around any individual motivation. So, keep reading!

Each motivation section has all the games that are centered around that particular motivation in one place. Then each section (except Sensory Hocus Pocus) is further divided into four sections, called Be it, Make it/Draw it, Showtime it and Superfact it.

Be it

Each "Be it" section has three different game ideas on how you can become the human version of that particular motivation. Remember, "Become the motivation itself" is part of Magic Ingredient 1.

You can do all three! Or just pick one. It's up to you. Do them exactly as they are written or modify them in a way that you think your child will particularly enjoy. That is the beauty of all the games in this book; they are open to be customized to your child or adult's interests and developmental stage. I walk you through how to do that in the next part of this chapter.

Make it/Draw it

This section includes games that involve us making a prop or craft or drawing something. You either do this before you introduce the game or activity to your child or adult, or with them. That will be your decision.

Showtime it

This includes games where we are performing, singing, dancing. I name it "Showtime it" as it reminds me of a Broadway show. If we want to become part of the game, we must unpack our performing skills and let our light shine brightly. Full disclosure, I cannot sing! I really mean it; if I sing alone, I pretty much have no chance of singing in tune. My friends always tease me that I make up a new tune for every song. But that does not stop me singing with the children and adults I work with. Many of our loved ones on the spectrum love music and songs. Remember, nobody else is watching or listening, just the child or adult, and they won't judge you.

In this category, there are games that include us becoming different people, such as pilots, princesses, animals, tour guides and train conductors. So, dust off those acting skills as well; allow yourself to dive deeply into your character acting skills. This is going to be fun!

Superfact it

This section is primarily for teenagers and adults on the spectrum who are fluently verbal. That is not to say you cannot use some of the games in the other sections, it just means that I have dedicated this section to that population. I chose the words "Superfact it" because a lot of our children and adults are really motivated by facts and knowing everything they can about a particular subject. They often love to discuss and talk about the subject a lot! This is not something to stop or move away from, but to embrace. I have utilized this motivation and passion to come up with different games and ideas to grow their interactive skills.

I hope that breaking it down into these four categories will help you find it easier to brainstorm your own new games. Now, when you are mulling over what to play you can think, okay, how can I:

- be it
- make it/draw it
- showtime it
- superfact it?

This gives you a starting place that will help you create your own interactive game.

How to modify each game to suit your child or adult's motivations and developmental stage

In this section, I will illustrate how you can modify a game easily and quickly to suit your child or adult on the spectrum. Once you get the hang of doing this, it opens up all the games in this book to your child or adult. That is a lot of games and activities, and it's going to take you a long time before you run out of ideas!

Modifying the game to a particular motivation

Here is the "Make a Giant Letter on the Floor" activity. Here is how it appears in the Letters motivation chapter in Part 2:

MAKE A GIANT LETTER ON THE FLOOR

- Get some artist tapes.
- With the tape make a giant letter on the floor—it could be any letter.
- Let it be as giant as you can make it, as big as the floor space is.

Maybe you want to play this game, but letters are not your child or adult's motivation. Easy solution, just swop out the letter for their actual motivation. For example, if they love dinosaurs, tape a dinosaur shape to the floor. If they like vacuum cleaners, tape a vacuum shape to the floor. Or the taped shape could be an animal or a guitar or a whole word instead of one letter.

Let's do the same with the "Make Alphabet Soup" activity. Here is how it appears in the Letters chapter:

MAKE ALPHABET SOUP

- Type out five of each letter of the alphabet.
- Space them so that you can cut them out so that each letter will be about the size of a postage stamp.
- Print the letters.
- Cut out the letters.
- Get a jug.
- Get two bowls, one for each of you.
- You have alphabet soup.
- You could also use plastic letters or Scrabble letter tiles.

If letters are not your child or adult's motivation, swop out the alphabet for spiders or helicopters. Yes, helicopters! You could print out lots of helicopter emojis and have helicopter soup that makes you fly around the room. Are you brave enough to eat spider soup? We will have to find out. But I think you are getting the idea.

How to modify the game to your child or adult's developmental stage

In talking about developmental stage I am focusing on two things: their interactive attention span (see Chapter 1) and their verbal communication ability. Remember, do not get confused between attention span and interactive attention span. To refresh your memory, attention span is just your child or adult's ability to engage with an object or toy. As we know, our children and adults are very skilled at this, and most have a concentration way beyond their peers. Interactive attention span is their ability to engage in an interaction with another person. This may include objects of course, but it also includes exchanges with another person, such as turn-taking, facial expressions, nonverbal communicative gestures and eye contact. Their interactive attention span could be anywhere from around 15 seconds to 20 minutes or more. It is basically the time they spend in the green-light zone.

Some of you may be thinking, but my child or adult's interactive attention span is so small—20–30 seconds—is it even worth presenting my game to them? I say a resounding "Yes!" Without a shadow of a doubt. That 20–30 seconds is our window to show our children what fun it is in our world. What delights we have to offer them. The more we show them what fun they could be having with us, the more reasons we give them to stay a little longer in the green light. Every second they do matters!

If you are holding a weight for two seconds and it is heavy for you, every time you do that you are building up the muscle—no one would say to you, "Ah don't bother, because unless you can hold it for more than five minutes it's not worth it." No, they don't, because every second you hold a heavy weight is building your muscle. It is the same with our children and adults, but we are building their interactive muscle instead. Let's start where they are and help them build it stronger.

How to modify the game based on your child/adult's interactive attention span

So, let's first look at how we can modify the game based on the length of our child or adult's interactive attention span. To illustrate this, I will use the "Horse Barn Game." Here is how it appears in the Animals and Insects chapter in Part 2:

HORSE BARN GAME

- Make a big barn for the horse.
- The barn is just two old sheets draped across furniture to create a den or fort.
- Put some yellow tissue/crepe paper on the floor as fake straw.
- Put some real or fake carrots and apples at the barn entrance in a bucket.
- Make some horse jumps out of bricks around the room.
- Get on all fours.
- Put a blanket on your back as a saddle.

- Neigh and trot around so that it is clear that you are a horse.
- Trot into the barn.
- Stick your head out and pretend to eat the carrots and apples just like a horse would.
- Come out again and do the horse jumps.

As you can see, there are many steps to this game. If your child or adult has an interactive attention span of over seven minutes, then it would be great to use all these steps. However, if they have a smaller attention span, I would take only one or two steps at a time.

For example, you could just do being a horse and going into the barn, then coming out again and eating a carrot. Or you could just put a saddle on your back and give them a horse ride. Or just jump over one jump.

The exciting thing is that when you do that you turn one game into four separate games. Abracadabra!

The longer their interactive attention span is, the more steps you can use in the game. Let the game inspire you to add your own steps.

Let's do it again with the "Weather Symbols Game." Here is how it appears in the Weather chapter in Part 2:

WEATHER SYMBOLS GAME

- Print and cut out weather symbols—clouds, clouds with rain, rain, lightning, wind and sun. To do this, just type "weather symbols" into an internet search engine and you will find a whole bunch of them.
- You will need three of each symbol.
- Collect the following items:
  - A bag of cotton balls. These will be clouds.
  - Aluminum foil. Cut the foil into strips. Make at least six strips. This will be the lightning.
  - A water squirter—but not in the shape of a gun. This will be the rain.
  - A flashlight. This will be the sun.
  - A handheld paper fan, or something you can use as a fan. This will be the wind.

- Sunglasses for when the sun comes out.
- An umbrella to put up when it rains.
- Tape all the weather symbols to yourself.
- Pull one off, hold it up and say its name. Then, if it is the:
  - sun—shine the flashlight
  - cloud—throw some cotton balls in the air
  - rain—use the water squirter
  - lightning—make the sound of thunder and then throw the lightning tin foil strips into the air
  - wind—use the fan to create wind.
- Keep doing that until all the weather symbols have been done.
- Then stick them all back on and repeat.

As you can see, there are five weather symbols to stick onto your shirt. If your child or adult has a shorter interactive attention span, just start with one or two symbols. If your child or adult has a longer one, you could even add more symbols to the shirt.

How to modify the game based on your child or adult's verbal communication level

You would modify this by adjusting the "Things you could invite your child/adult to do" section of the game to more fully reflect their individual verbal abilities and challenges.

To illustrate this, let's use the "Wish Upon a Star Game" from the games in Part 2 for motivations that are to do with watching things dangle, drop or spin:

WISH UPON A STAR GAME

- Cut out star shapes.
- Attach long pieces of ribbon to the stars.
- They are shooting stars.
- Throw them in the air across the room.
- Make at least four, so you can put on a Wish Upon a Star show, by throwing them one after the other.
- Repeat.

Things you could invite your child/adult to do

- Watch you throw the stars.
- Say, "throw," "star" or any version of that.
- Pick up the stars and give to you to throw them again.
- Throw the stars themselves.
- Make the stars with you.
- Make a wish before they throw the stars.

In the "Things you could invite your child/adult to do" section you will see there are two ideas on how you could challenge your child or adult to verbally participate. The first one, "Say, 'throw,' 'star' or any version of that" is asking them to say just one word. This is great for a child or adult who has a small vocabulary, or who is not using their single words consistently in a functional way or has yet to say a word.

The way you would modify the game is to come up with verbal challenges that meet your child or adult where they are and slightly lift them to the next verbal stage. For example, if your child or adult can already talk in a three-word sentence, you might invite them to speak in a four-word sentence. That could be, "Throw another big star" or "Throw in the air." If your child or adult can speak in sentences but has challenges answering questions, you could ask them a question. One question could be, "How many stars shall I throw in the air?" If your child or adult is fully fluent, you might say something that will enhance their conversational skills, such as, "Let's think of a wish we have and tell each other before I throw the next shooting star."

Think of what you want to verbally invite them to do as you prepare the game, so if you get a chance you will be ready with the invitation.

A quick note on imagination play

I have written quite a few games that include imaginary play. I strongly suggest you use and introduce these types of games to your child or adult even if they have not yet responded to or shown an ability to play imagination games or engage in symbolic play. I say this for the following reasons:

1. Just because your child or adult has not shown a capability to do or understand imaginary play does not mean that they do

not or cannot. It is vital to remember that a lack of response does not mean a lack of understanding.

2. If your child or adult does have trouble understanding the concept of imaginary play, that is precisely the reason why adding an imaginary element to the game is highly beneficial to them. This gives them exposure to it. How can they learn about something if it is never offered or modeled to them? We can model and teach them step by step.

3. They are fun for you. They add a richness to your game playing that will help you be more interesting and more playful. The more richness we have and the more stimulation our children or adults have, the more opportunity they have to learn and grow. The more fun we have, the more enticing we become at inspiring them to interact.

A quick note about age

Let's not get caught in a limiting paradigm about what is age appropriate and what is not. For Easter, I gave my 20-year-old niece a little soft bunny. I also gave her some stylish clothes. While she did like the stylish clothes and was grateful, she jumped up and down and squealed with delight when she saw the cute little bunny. One of my close friends was having a challenging time and feeling very lonely and isolated so I sent her a plush bulldog. It became her companion and helped her get through this difficult time. Another friend in his fifties will only watch animated movies that have PG ratings. There are grown men who spend hours playing video games or coveting and polishing their vintage plastic toy figurines. A large proportion of perfectly intelligent adults love silly and ridiculous movies. We love what we love. That is more important than what is age appropriate.

Having said that, you always want to talk to your child or adult at the level that their age is. If I am working with a 20-year-old, I will talk to them as a person who has had 20 years of experience and development, regardless of their language communication level. (That's why it would be great to introduce some of the topics from the "Superfact it" section to our not yet verbal adults and teenagers.) If I am talking to a three-year-old, I will talk about a three-year-old's subjects and at their cognitive level.

Please also remember that the "Superfact it" section has games topics that are designed for teenagers and adults on the spectrum who have mostly fluent verbal communication skills.

If you think your child or adult is not motivated by any toy or object

There are many children and adults on the spectrum who are "sensory seekers." This may mean that it "seems" to you that your child or adult is not interested or motivated by any toys, characters, books or objects but instead is:

- very sedentary or lying down for a large proportion of the time
- in perpetual motion
- intermittently throughout the day doing one or more of the following:
  - running
  - jumping
  - swinging
  - climbing
  - rocking
  - chewing
  - tapping the walls
  - tapping their mouth
  - tapping their head
  - slapping the walls or floor
  - slapping the side of their legs, their head or chest
  - head banging
  - hand biting
  - foot stomping
  - hand clapping.

Sensory seeking just means that your child or adult is doing something to their body to give themselves a sensory experience that is helpful to their sensory and nervous systems.

A lot of sensory seekers have "hyposensitivity," which means that they are under-sensitive to input. This explains why so many of our children or adults really enjoy deep pressure on their hands, or feet and head. Some of you may know that your child likes to bury their head or chin into you. My god-daughter Jade would do what I called "chinning."

She would press her chin into my leg or arm or against my chin so hard that it would hurt. Of course, this was totally unintentionally on her part; she was just seeking the sensory pressure that she needed. To help her with this, I showed her how she could press her chin into the palm of my hand and then I would put my other hand on top of her head and squeeze it very strongly. She loved this! It became a frequent activity between us.

I share this with you to illustrate that although it seems your child or adult does not have a motivation, they do. It isn't a thing; it is sensory input itself. That *is* the motivation. With Jade I used her motivation for sensory input on her chin to maximize the amount of interaction we could have together by providing her myself with the sensory input she was seeking. I was "being it" for her, in the way I talk about for Magic Ingredient 1 (see Chapter 1). Each time she wanted the pressure, she knew she could come to me for it. This created more interactive attention span, eye contact and verbal communication opportunities.

Bouncing on a trampoline or on a therapy ball is something that some of our children and adults on the spectrum love to do. I have worked with many a child/adult whose main motivation was to bounce themselves on a therapy ball. If they are not bouncing on a trampoline or therapy ball they are jumping on the floor or bouncing themselves in a kneeling position on the floor. In the sensory world, bouncing as well as swinging stimulates the vestibular sensory system. Our children and adults are in some sense giving themselves their own occupational therapy. We don't want to stop that; let's help them with it and at the same time strengthen their interactive and social skills. We can do that by including ourselves and creating games around this sensory motivation.

The final set of games and activities presented in Part 2 have been designed especially around the motivation of sensory input. I call them Sensory Hocus Pocus and have divided them into sensory input categories:

- Squeezes/massage
- Clapping/tapping
- Swinging/spinning
- Full body input
- Perpetual motion: rides
- Hurdles, jumps and running
- Bouncing.

For many of the games I have offered variations so that they will be suitable for children of different ages or for adults, for example the "Piggyback Ride Game" and "Office Chair Ride Game." I hope you will find some activities that will suit your child or adult's sensory motivation and enable you to have some fun interaction with your loved one.

Read all of the games in this book

You now know how to modify these games to suit your child or adult. So do read all the games in this book. Not only can you modify each one to play with your individual child or adult but doing so will help you to come up with new and different games. I have written this book not only to give you ideas, but also to inspire you to be able to tailor-make your own games. Reading all of them will help you in this process.

A note about preparation time

As I designed these activities, I have kept in mind the tight schedules that you are all on. A game or activity is not useful to you if it takes too much time to create. The activities in this book range from about three to 20 minutes' preparation time, with most of them being on the lower end of that.

However, let's talk about ways that you can delegate this prep time. When Jade's (my goddaughter) parents were running her Son-Rise Program, they worked and had a baby son. So, time was tight! One thing they became familiar with was asking for help and delegating. When Jade got to the point where she was ready to transition to school, we began home schooling her to catch her up academically. At that time, home schooling involved a lot of preparation. Although the classes were written out for us, we had to gather and cut and stick and everything else in between! Bryn (her mom) and I would get together every Sunday night and prepare all the week's classes. This saved a lot of time and was fun social time for Bryn and me. I suggest you do something similar. Do you have older children or nieces and nephews who can print and cut out pictures and prepare activities from this book? All you would have to do is pick the activities you want to try, and they do the rest. As a little bit of incentive, they could earn some pocket money. Or do what Bryn did and invite your friends over for a prepping party. You provide the snacks; they provide their hands. Activities would get prepared in no time.

A little note for all those perfectionists reading this: do not get too caught up in preparing perfectly. When you are cutting out pictures, you do not have to cut perfectly around the edges—it takes too long. When you draw something, it does not have to be a work of art. Good enough is the new great. The magic comes from the magic ingredients not from what the props look like. Nowhere in the Magic Ingredients did I say that things have to look great.

Materials

Essential materials

I would suggest that you definitely make sure you have or start collecting the following items:

- Poster boards
- Colored paper/card
- Artist/masking/builders tape—it is called different things in different countries
- Copy paper
- A printer and a computer. If you do not have one, that is okay; you can go to your local library or use a friend's
- Crepe paper
- Tissue paper
- Markers/colored pencils
- String
- Regular tape
- Boxes—start saving and collecting cereal boxes, toilet rolls, Amazon boxes, plastic bottles and so on
- Giant boxes—you can get these from your local appliance store. They are usually very willing to get rid of them
- Popsicle sticks
- Roll of butcher paper.

Below is a long list of all the materials you would use if you were to make everything for the 180+ activities in this book. However, I want to add that I have also mentioned in the activity sections a lot of alternative household objects you could use instead. For example, instead of using a toy microphone use a spoon or a pen.

ART AND CRAFTS

- Artist/builders' tape
- Big ball of ribbon
- Calligraphy pen
- Colored markers/pencils
- Crepe paper—all colors but particularly yellow, green and blue
- Fun stickers of anything
- Giant, big and small cardboard boxes
- Nontoxic face paints
- Popsicle/lollipop sticks—a big packet
- Poster board
- Printed out pictures of family members and friends
- Roll of butcher paper
- Strong masking tape
- Tissue paper—all colors but particularly yellow, green and blue.

CLOTHES

- Dressing-up clothes:
  - Crown
  - Tiara
  - Superman cape
  - Cat ears and tail
  - Wigs
- Four belts
- Two silk or silk-like scarfs
- Hat you can safety pin a sign to and wear yourself
- Sunglasses.

CLASSROOM/OFFICE ITEMS

- Books (*any that you or your child has*)
- Handheld small whiteboard
- Handheld small chalk board

- Hole puncher
- One pack of colored card (*regular size*)
- One pack of colored paper (*regular size*)
- Plain small circle sticker that you can write on
- Printer
- Regular cheap printing paper
- Two packs of index/revision cards.

HOUSEHOLD OBJECTS

- Blanket
- Broom or mop
- Catalog with pictures of toilets, vacuums, blenders and other household objects
- Cotton wool
- Envelopes
- Garbage trash bags
- Handheld paper fan
- Holiday decorations
- Kitchen aluminum
- Laundry basket
- Old camcorder
- Old cell phone cases
- Old magazines and newspapers
- Old sheets
- Old TV remote
- 20 paper plates
- Plastic bags
- Plastic plates, bowls, cups and a jug
- Pile of clothes (*any size or kind*)
- Regular Scotch tape
- Safety pin
- String
- Three household buckets
- Two small handheld flashlights
- Umbrella
- Wooden spoon.

SPORTING/GAMES EQUIPMENT

- Big therapy ball
- Child's racket/bat of some sort
- Drums
- 20 ping pong balls
- Frisbee
- Long sticks you find outside
- One regular pack of cards
- Scrabble letter pieces
- Sling shot
- Small ball that bounces
- Tennis ball
- Triangle
- Two big hula hoops.

TOYS

- Balloons (*not blown up*)
- Figurines of any kind
- Lego
- Letter blocks
- Plastic letters and numbers
- Pretend food
- Puppets (*any kind but preferably with big mouths*)
- Stuffed animals and baby dolls (*if they are talking ones, take the batteries out of them*)
- Three stuffed animals or figures of pigs and frogs
- Toy helicopter (*not battery operated*)
- Toy microphone
- Toy rocket
- Toy vehicles, of any kind (*not battery operated*)
- Wagon that you pull
- Water squirter.

CHAPTER 4

Demystifying the Process

As a way to demystify the game-playing process I have taken one of the games and broken it down step by step, sharing not only how your child or adult might respond to the game but my thought process and responses as well.

As we never know how they might react, I have mentioned here a few of the most common possibilities. Examples include a child who already has some verbal communication skills and a child who has not yet spoken. There are five examples with a three-, six-, ten-, 14- and 25-year-old. Please read all the examples. I believe you will get more from this book if you do.

For this purpose, I am going to use the "Number Plate Game" from the Numbers chapter in Part 2.

NUMBER PLATE GAME

- Get a bunch of cheap paper plates—around 20 of them.
- Excitedly take them out and write a number on each plate, 1–20.
- Once you have written a number on the plate, toss it on the floor. The number does not have to fall in order on the floor. Toss them here, there and everywhere.

Things you can do with the number plates

- Jump on all the prime numbers.
- Hop onto number 1, then say, "Where is number 2?" Then jump to 2, then say, "Where is number 3?" and then hop to 3, until you have done all the numbers.
- Say the 2 times table while stepping on the plates with 2, 4, 6, 8 and so on.
- Get a ball and say, "I am going to make this land on number 7." Shout out another number and throw the ball onto that number plate. Keep going with all the numbers.
- Draw one object on the number 1 plate, two objects on the number 2 plate and so forth for all the numbers.
- Pick up all the plates and throw them into the air like unidentified flying saucers.
- Try anything else you can think of.

Things you could invite your child/adult to do

- Tell you what number to write on the plate.
- Throw a number plate onto the floor.
- Watch you write the numbers.
- Help you write the numbers on the plates.
- Jump or hop on the numbers with you.
- Jump on each number you call out.
- Tell you which number to jump or hop on.
- Point to where each number is so that you can jump onto them.
- Make each plate fly in the air like a Frisbee.
- Watch you throwing the plates in the air like a Frisbee.
- Play Frisbee with you with the plates.

You have three sections: the structure of the game itself, the many different things you can do with the numbered paper plates and the things you could invite your child to do in the game itself. This structure for each game will:

- accommodate as much as possible the uniqueness of every child and adult

- help you see all the different things you can do and invite them to do within just one game
- get your creative juices flowing and inspire you to come up with even more ideas for this game or for using paper plates in other games
- encourage you to leave room for the unplanned bit (Magic Ingredient 4).

Play by play 1: With Fatima, a not yet verbal three-year-old on the spectrum

Before playing the game with Fatima I must do the following tasks:

- Prepare the game so that I have everything I need. In this case, it is just the 20 paper plates and a marker to write the numbers with.
- Look over the "Things you can do with the number plates" section and either choose one or a few from the suggestions that I think are fun or make up something else that I think Fatima would enjoy doing.
- Look over the "Things you could invite your child/adult to do" section so I have a few ideas to mind if I get the opportunity to ask her to participate with me in the game.
- Prepare my mind and make sure I am holding the top five "Presto Chango" beliefs:
  - 1. I am creative and can make anything fun!
  - 2. My child or adult will find this interesting!
  - 3. I can have fun even if my child or adult does not respond in any clear way.
  - 4. My attempt *is* the success!
  - 5. My child or adult's response is *not* a statement about my parenting, my skill, how interesting I am or how successful I was with my child/adult.

  By "prepare" I mean I set the intention to come from these beliefs while I am with Fatima. I will even meditate on them for a minute. I am always amazed at the magic of centering myself in this way and how just one minute really makes a difference.

Playing the game with Fatima

- I observe Fatima for red lights and green lights.
- When I see a green-light opportunity, I think to myself, "This is the moment I get to initiate the game and feel excited to offer this fun game."
- I celebrate the green light, in this case it is eye contact, by verbally saying, "I love that you are looking straight into my eyes. Your eyes are beautiful, Fatima!"
- After that celebration, I observe her again to make sure that she is still in a green light.
- She is, so I know for certain that it is a good time to introduce the "Number Plate Game."
- I immediately get a paper plate and write the number 1 on it. I hold it up so that Fatima can see and toss it onto the floor. It lands near her feet.
- I quickly do another plate, writing the number 2 on it. I hold it up so that she can see, and toss it into the air. I sing the number 2 in an operatic voice.
- I write another; this time I whisper the number 3 and show it her and toss it into the air in a different direction from the first two.
- This has taken maybe 30 seconds to do and Fatima is still looking at me and the plates.
- I celebrate her for looking at me and watching the plates.
- I write the number 5 on a plate, toss it into the air and this one goes over her head and lands behind her. I laugh a little. She turns to see where it lands. She looks back at me. Then she starts shaking her piece of string and looking at it; her green light has turned to red.
- Seeing her red light, I stop playing the game. As I stop playing the game, I am feeling good that she is in a red light and able to regulate herself in this way, and awesome that she looked at me, the game and showed enjoyment in what I was offering for over half a minute! For the developmental stage that Fatima is in right now, this is great! For over half a minute she has worked her spontaneous eye contact, her interactive attention span and

her interest in another person's activity. I am glad that I had something to offer her for the time she was able to connect.

- I also think to myself, as she has shown enjoyment and interest in this activity, I will introduce it again if she gives another green light.
- As she is in a red light, I join her in her red light. (To learn more about red lights and joining please see the Recommended Reading and Resources section at the back of this book.) For now, you can just wait for the next green light.

Play by play 2: With Billy, a not yet verbal ten-year-old on the spectrum

Before playing the game with Billy I prepare in the same way as I did for Fatima (see above).

Playing the game with Billy

- I observe Billy for red lights and green lights.
- When I see a green-light opportunity, I think to myself, "This is the moment I get to initiate the game and feel excited to offer this fun game."
- Knowing that green lights are challenging for Billy, I celebrate the green light. In this case, it is eye contact, so I sincerely say, "Thank you for looking at me. That lets me know you might be interested in playing with me."
- After that celebration, I observe him again to make sure that he is still in a green light.
- He is, so I know for certain that it is a good time to introduce the "Number Plate Game."
- I immediately get a paper plate and write the number 1 on it. I hold it up so that he can see and toss it onto the floor; it lands to his right.
- I quickly do another plate, writing the number 2 on it. I hold it up so that he can see, and toss it into the air, saying the number 2 excitedly.
- I do plates number 3 and 4.

- After plate number 4, Billy gets up and gathers all the plates together and places them on the floor in a row. He then looks up at me.
- I celebrate him looking at me and write number 5 on a plate and toss it in the air.
- He runs over to it and puts it in his number plate line up.
- This is where I think of Magic Ingredient 4, "The magic of the unplanned." The game is not about putting the numbers in a row, but this is what Billy wants to do so it is now a great part of the game.
- After he puts it in his row he looks up at me again. I celebrate him; this time I say, "Thanks for looking at me to show me you are ready for another plate."
- I sing as I write the number 6 on the plate and hold it up to show him. Only this time I do not toss it, I dance over to him and put it neatly in his row. This is my way of including his awesome addition to the game. The added bonus is that as I dance over to him, he looks at me for longer than if I had tossed it into the air. (Note: so far, I have not asked him to do anything, but he is working on his interactive attention span and his eye contact just because I introduced a game that was centered around his interests and involved me—and used Magic Ingredient 4.)
- I do the same thing for plates 6, 7, 8 and 9.
- It is clear he is really enjoying this game and wants it to continue. Because he is so motivated, I know it is time to ask him to become more involved. He is physically involved in the game and looking at me, so I decide to ask him to verbally participate. I want to give him the opportunity to practice saying a word. He likes me dancing the plates over to him, so I decide to ask him to say the word "dance."
- To make this easier for him, I say the word "dance" many times as I dance over plate numbers 10, 11 and 12.
- When I get to plate 13, just before I am going to dance over to him, I stop and say, "If you want me to dance, say dance." Then I pause and give him the time to say the word. He says a sound, "ahahah." I cheer that sound and dance over with the plate.
- I do the same for plates 14 and 15. He says the sound each time. I celebrate his attempt each time.

- Then his green light turns red.
- Wow! That is about six minutes of interaction. I know he has worked hard and needs a break. I am glad that he knows how to regulate himself. I joyfully join him in his red light and know that there is a lot more room left to play with the "Number Plate Game" when he is next in a green light.
- For six minutes he has spontaneously worked on his interactive attention span and his eye contact and verbal communication! Go, Billy, go!

Play by play 3: With Leon, a verbal six-year-old on the spectrum

Before playing the game with Leon I prepare in the same way as I did for Fatima (see above).

Playing the game with Leon

- I observe Leon for red and green lights.
- He comes over to me and sits on my lap and hooks his arm affectionately around my head. This is a green light. I celebrate him, saying, "I love it when you come over and sit with me."
- After my celebration of his green light I observe him again to make sure he is in a green light. He is. Aha! Time to introduce my great game.
- I stand up with him still in my arms and say, "I have a great game to show you." I go over (while holding him on my hip) and get the plates and the pen and sit with him at the table. He is still sitting on my lap, and now he is curiously looking at the paper plates.
- I write number 1 on one plate. He says, "1." I cheer him and say, "Yes, it's number 1." I toss the plate onto the floor. Leon then says, "No," and runs and gets it and puts it back on the table. Then hops back on my lap.
- I cheer him and say, "Thanks for letting me know that you don't want me to toss the plates on the floor."
- I then use a component from Magic Ingredient 1, "Become

super useful." I make a mental note never to toss the plates on the floor again. That part of the game is off limits; it is more important that I show that I am really listening to Leon than it is that I toss the plates. There are so many other things I can do with the plates on the table. (That is one of the reasons why the games I have created are open-ended.)

- Then I write number 2 on the next plate; he says, "2." I cheer him again for saying 2 and leave plate number 2 on the table.

- I draw number 3; he looks at me and says, "3." I cheer him for looking at me and talking.

- Then he looks at me and says, "4," so I cheer him and tell him that I would love to write number 4, so I do.

- We do this all the way to 20 plates! Looking, talking, smiling with one another—seven whole minutes of interaction.

- He is still enjoying sitting on my lap and in a green light, so I take plate number 1 and say, "One dog," and draw a dog on the plate. Leon looks at me and barks. I laugh and bark with him.

- I take the number 2 plate and draw two pigs. Leon then snorts twice.

- I decide to challenge him to answer a question. I know answering questions is a challenge for him, so it is great to ask him one here while he is so motivated by this game, creating a positive association in his brain with being asked a question.

- The next plate is number 3. I pause and say, "What three things shall I draw on this plate?"

- He looks at me and is quiet for about five seconds then says, "Balloons." I cheer his brilliant idea and draw three balloons.

- I do not want to bombard him with many questions all in a row, so I come up with the next one. I model the question to myself by saying out loud, "What four things shall I draw on this plate?" And then answer it with tigers. I draw four tigers; he growls.

- Then for number 5, I ask him, "What five things shall I draw on this plate?" He pauses for about 30 seconds this time and then says, "5." I cheer him and say, "Yes, what five things shall I draw?" He pauses again and then says, "Cats," so I cheer him and draw five cats. He watches me draw the cats as he meows away.

- After that his green light turns red. We have played and talked and looked at each other and he has even answered some questions. What great interaction from a fun game! He has worked his interactive attention span for ten minutes. He has made spontaneous eye contact and worked his functional verbal communication. He is a star!

Play by play 4: With Lilly, a fluently verbal 14-year-old on the spectrum

Before playing the game with Lilly I prepare in the same way as I did for Fatima (see above).

Playing the game with Lilly

- I observe Lilly for red and green lights.
- She says to me, "Kate, what did you bring today?"
- I celebrate this question, which is a clear green light. I say, "That's pretty great that you asked me that and are interested in what I might have brought. You are an awesome friend."
- Then I answer her question. I say, "I will show you."
- Before I can show her, she replies, "No, I don't want to play it." I say, "That's okay, you don't have to play it; I will just show you it."
- To which she replies, "No, don't."
- I say, "Okay, you are so clear in telling me what you want, I like that about you." I feel really happy that she can tell me what she wants and does not want; that is a great skill. I am happy that I can be responsive to her and let her know that people listen and that her language is powerful.
- She says, "Thanks," and then the green light turns into a red light.
- I gladly join her in the red light. (For now, you can just wait and observe her until the next green light.)
- I am pleased that I can give her a positive experience of someone listening to her and enjoying even her "No"s, knowing that not pushing my game and respecting her communication and her need for the red light will pave a way for more opportunities

DEMYSTIFYING THE PROCESS   85

to play that game or another game later, when she is ready. She has also worked her conversation skills as we had a successful three-loop conversation.

- I have engaged "Presto Chango" Belief 4, "My attempt *is* the success," and 5, "My child/adult's response is *not* a statement about my parenting, my skill, how interesting I am or how successful I was with my child/adult."

Play by play 5: With Yeshu, a not yet verbal 25-year-old on the spectrum

Before playing the game with Yeshu I prepare in the same way as I did for Fatima (see above).

Playing the game with Yeshu

- I observe Yeshu for red and green lights.
- He starts to look at my game bag and then at me and then at the bag. He comes over to the bag and touches it and then looks at me.
- I celebrate his green light of eye contact and his nonverbal gestures which I interpret as curiosity about what is in the bag.
- After my celebration, I observe Yeshu again to make sure he is still in a green light; he is.
- I ask him if he wants to see what's inside. He nods. I celebrate this awesome nonverbal answer. I think to myself that it is time to initiate the "Number Plate Game."
- I have a choice to make here. As he is so interested in my bag, I could tell him to open it up himself and have a look. Or I could take the game out myself. Because I want to use Magic Ingredient 1 and have a role in the game, I choose the latter and take the game out myself. This gives me a role in the game and encourages more spontaneous eye contact and nonverbal gestures.
- I take out the paper plates and the markers and immediately write the number 1 on the plate in the color purple. I know

Yeshu loves numbers and loves purple. I toss the plate onto the floor.

- I take another plate and write the number 2 on it and toss it onto the floor again. Yeshu smiles, takes a plate and my purple pen and starts writing the number 1 on the plate and tosses it like I had.
- I celebrate him.
- We both write numbers on the plates and look at each other. After Yeshu tosses his plate he gets up to go over to it and point at it and wave me to come see it. I happily hop up to see his plate. Taking his enjoyment of showing me where his landed as a cue, I go over to mine and beckon him over, using the words, "Come and see mine." He comes over to mine. Then we go back and write numbers together on our plates, and then go and look where they have landed. We do this until all the plates are done.
- Once they are all done, I observe him to make sure he is still in a green light—he is! So I challenge him further by suggesting the next step in the game. I point to his number 1 and say, "Step on the 1." Then I point to his plate 2 and challenge him to jump from his 1 to his 2. This type of physical activity is challenging for Yeshu, but he does it. Then I stand on my plate 1 and jump to my plate 2. Then I say, "Let's jump to number 3," and I jump. He watches me and then he does it. We jump together all the way to number 11.
- At number 11, after 15 minutes of interactive playing, I observe his green light turn red. Noticing this, I stop encouraging the game and join him in his red light. (For now, you can just wait and observe him until the next green light.)
- He has lengthened his interactive attention span, worked his spontaneous eye contact and nonverbal communication, taken turns and practiced writing numbers! What amazing work, Yeshu!

Now you have a clearer idea on how to play these games, I am excited for you to turn the page, choose a game from Part 2 and then, of course, play it with your lovely child or adult. Remember, there are no wrong moves and no wrong responses from either you or them. Have fun, and don't forget the five Presto Chango beliefs (see Chapter 2).

THE GAMES
AND ACTIVITIES

Letters

BE IT

VERSION 1

- Print out a picture of a keyboard.
- Tape it to a poster board.
- Get some string and attach a loop to the top of the poster board so that it can go over your head. You have become a human keyboard.

VERSION 2

- Write a single capital letter on a piece of paper, tape it or safety pin it to your shirt. You are that letter.
- Act out everything that begins with that letter. For example, here are some things to act out if you chose the letter "C":
  - Cat
  - Cartwheel
  - Carnival
  - Carnivore
  - Camper bus
  - Curiosity
  - Curls
  - Canine
  - Candy

- Candy floss
- Camping
- Chameleon
- Carnation
- Crab.
- Don't forget you can do this with every letter of the alphabet!

VERSION 3

- Hide magnetic letters all over your body in your clothes. You can hide them:
  - under your shirt
  - in your pocket
  - in your socks
  - in your shoes
  - in your waistband
  - under your cuffs
  - under your sweater on each of your shoulders.
- Keep finding them and presenting them to your child/ adult in fun and dynamic ways. You could say:
  - "Ta-da—the letter A comes to you from my shoulder."
  - "Letter O comes to you from my toe" (to a drum roll).
  - "Letter P comes to you from my sleeve" (as you spin in a circle).

Abracadabra! That's three different ways to become letters of the alphabet.

Things you can do once you have become a keyboard or a letter

For Version 1

- Type out the alphabet on the keyboard.
- Type out different body parts and point to them.
- Type out different animal words and become that animal.

- Type out a different song title and then sing that song.
- Type random letters and say them in varying funny voices. For example:
  - high and squeaky
  - low and growly
  - in the voice of Mickey Mouse or Daffy Duck
  - in a whisper.
- Type out a fun story (remember you can use one you already know and your child/adult likes).
- Type out words in "Martian" language, or another language.
- Type out magic spells.

For Version 3

Once you find and present a letter that was hidden on you:

- Chase your child/adult with it.
- Throw it in the air.
- Throw it at a therapy ball or mini trampoline and watch it jump in the air.
- Give it to your child/adult.
- Pretend to eat the letter: "Ooh—Y is yummy, but G is gross, and P is peculiar!"

Things you could invite your child/adult to do

For Version 1

- Type a letter on your letter board.
- Type a sentence of something they want you to do for them or get for them.
- Instead of talking, decide you are going to communicate to each other just by typing on the keyboard. It's a keyboard conversation.
- Create their own keyboard pasteboard to wear.
- Watch you type on your keyboard.

For Version 2

- Act out a word that starts with the letter you are wearing, and you guess what it is.
- Tell you what new letter to become.
- Write a letter and tape it to you.
- Watch you act out the different words.

For Version 3

- Verbally guess where you have hidden a letter.
- Point to where you have hidden a letter.
- Name the letters you find.
- Come up with a word that begins with the letter you find.
- Spell a word or sentence with all the letters you find.
- Take from you the letters you find.
- Watch you find them.

MAKE IT/DRAW IT

MAKE A GIANT LETTER ON THE FLOOR

- Get some artist tape.
- With the tape, make a giant letter on the floor—it could be any letter.
- Let it be as giant as you can make it, as big as the floor space is.

Things you can do once you have made the letter

- Run along it saying the letter.
- Give your child a ride as you run along the letter.
- Drive a toy car or train along the letter.
- Let's say you made a giant letter B, then draw little "b"s all over the tape making the big B.
- Draw things that begin with "b" on the giant B.
- Draw eyes, a nose and a mouth on the giant B. Make it speak.

It could say "ouch" every time you stand on it. Or it could say words beginning with "b."

- Once you have played with one letter, make another.

Things you could invite your child/adult to do

- Tell you what letter to make next.
- Run along the letter themselves.
- Make a letter with the tape themselves.
- Roll a toy vehicle along it.
- Draw on it.
- Tell you words beginning with "b" to draw on the letter.
- Watch you as you make it or draw on it or run along it.

MAKE ALPHABET SOUP

- Type out five of each letter of the alphabet.
- Space them so that you can cut them out so that each letter will be about the size of a postage stamp.
- Print the letters.
- Cut out the letters.
- Get a jug.
- Get two bowls, one for each of you.
- You have alphabet soup.
- You could also use plastic letters or Scrabble letter tiles.

Things you can do once you have made the soup

- Simply pour it into the bowls in a fun and enthusiastic way.
- Sing the alphabet song as you pour the alphabet soup.
- Pretend to eat the soup.
- Set up a tea party to share your alphabet soup. Invite all the stuffed animals or figurines.
- Slurp loudly when you pretend to eat the soup.
- "Accidentally" pour the soup on your head.
- "Accidentally" pour the soup on your child/adult's head.

- Pick out different letters to spell a word and then eat that word.
- Each time you pretend to eat a mouthful of alphabet soup it makes you sing all the letters you just swallowed.
- Variations: Alphabet pasta or Alphabet chicken nuggets. Or take the letters and make them into a letter sandwich.

Things you could invite your child/adult to do

- Pour the soup into the bowls.
- Tell you who to invite to the tea party.
- Go and get a stuffed animal or figurine to sit at the table.
- Set the table for the tea party.
- Feed alphabet soup to the stuffed animal.
- Tell you what word to eat.
- Spell out a word to eat.
- Pretend to eat the soup.
- Make more letters for the soup.
- Watch you pour and eat the soup.

MAKE A TOWER OF LETTERS

- Get a bunch of letter blocks, plastic letters or Scrabble tiles.
- Make them into the highest tower you can.
- Then knock them down and start again.

Things you could invite your child/adult to do

- Build the tower with you.
- Give you a letter to build the tower.
- Tell you which letter to put on the tower next.
- Knock the tower over.
- Watch you build the tower and knock it over.

SHOWTIME IT

BALLOON LETTERS GAME

- Get a bunch of cheap balloons.
- Write a letter on each balloon.
- Blow them up so that your child/adult can see the letter get bigger and bigger.

Things you can do with the balloon letters

- Blow them up as your child/adult watches.
- Blow them up and let them go, so your child/adult gets the fun of watching the letter get bigger and bigger and watching the balloon deflate as it whizzes around the room.
- Blow them up and tie them so they stay full. When you have enough, spell out words or put them in alphabetical order.
- See how long you can keep the balloon in the air without it touching the floor.
- Play letter balloon volleyball.
- Rub the balloon on your clothes so it gets static and clings to you. See how many balloons you can attach to yourself that way.

Things you could invite your child/adult to do

- Hand you the balloon to blow up.
- Write a letter on the balloon.
- Tell you which letter to write on the balloon.
- Tell you which color balloon to blow up next.
- Bat the balloon back and forth to you as if it is a ball.
- Spell a word with all the balloon letters.
- Help you put all the balloons in alphabetical order.
- Draw a picture of something that begins with the letter that is on the balloon.
- Help you keep the balloon in the air.
- Give you the next balloon to blow up.
- Watch you blow up the balloons.

LETTER SHOW

- Pick one letter, any letter, let's say it is a "B."
- Find or make as many "B/b"s as you can:
  - Get both a plastic "b" and "B"
  - A card with the letter "b" on it
  - A Scrabble tile "B"
  - A "b" cut out from a newspaper/magazine
  - A giant "B" you drew on a poster board
  - Lots of "b"s you typed and printed out
  - A "b" that may be on a t-shirt
  - A "b" you drew on a handheld whiteboard or a chalk board
  - A piece of string you laid out on the floor in the shape of a "b/B."
- Announce that the "Letter of the Day" show is about to begin.
- Get a toy microphone or pretend that a pen is your microphone.
- In a fun voice, announce or sing, "Today we bring to you the letter B!"
- Present/draw all the different "b"s.
- You can continue with all the letters of the alphabet.

Things you could invite your child/adult to do

- Watch you present the letters.
- Bring one of their stuffed animals or figurine friends to watch with them.
- Say the letter.
- Point to the letter they want you to do next.
- Get a letter they want you to do next.
- Draw the letter.
- Sing the announcement song with you.

LETTER SONGS

- Sing one of the following letter songs:
  - BINGO—https://youtu.be/9mmF8zOlh_g
  - The ABC Song— https://youtu.be/75p-N9YKqNo.
  - The Letter A Song. It is simple and easy to learn. Adapt it to every letter of the alphabet. https://youtu.be/tFG_wchwpUk
  - YMCA—https://youtu.be/CS9OOOS5w2k
  - Act Out the Alphabet—https://youtu.be/dLReNTmMkKA

Note: These are for you to watch and learn the songs to sing to your child/adult, not for your child/adult to watch.

Things you can do when you are singing the songs

- Do all the actions as you sing.
- Draw the letters when you sing.

Things you could invite your child/adult to do

- Do one of the actions.
- Sing along.
- Draw the letter.
- Listen to you singing.
- Ask you to sing.
- Watch you sing.

SUPERFACT IT

RESEARCH INTERESTING FACTS ABOUT LETTERS

Here are some topics to try:

- Find out about as many different alphabets as you can.

For example, there are the Greek, Latin and Armenian alphabets.
- Who first invented the alphabet?
- Chinese characters. How do they differ?
- How many words begin with "B" in the English language. How many in French, Spanish and so on.
- How do crossword puzzle clues work?
- The history of codes using letters.
- Morse Code.
- The history of the written word. How did writing begin and evolve from pictures on cave walls to letters, to tablets, to paper, to books, to typewriters, to computers, to voice-activated software?

How you can use this information with your child/adult

Share it with your child/adult

- Have a conversation with your child/adult about it. Ask them what they think about the information you just gave them. Which alphabet do they like best; what was their favorite part? Do they agree or disagree with what you shared?
- Share it with them verbally.
- Give them articles to read.
- Sing it to them.
- Write it out on a whiteboard or a chalk board.

Morse Code Games

- Teach your child/adult the Morse Code.
- Communicate using only the taps of Morse Code.
- Use a flashlight to signal Morse Code:
  - Get two flashlights, one for you and one for your child/adult.
  - Turn off the lights.
  - Use only the flashes of Morse Code light to communicate.

Make a crossword full of your favorite words

- You could make this together as a project. Maybe a gift for a family member's birthday.
- You could create it yourself and have fun helping your child/ adult solve it.
- You could each make a small crossword and have each other do it.

Draw calligraphy

- Get pictures of calligraphy writing.
- Have fun trying to reproduce them.
- Make a menu for lunch/dinner in fancy calligraphy.
- Make table place settings for the whole family in calligraphy.
- Learn how to write fancy Chinese or Japanese characters:
    - Write out your names in Chinese/Japanese.
    - Think about a word that inspires each of you and write that out.

Name that Letter quiz

- Get a regular pack of cards.
- Take 20 of the cards.
- Print out different characters from different alphabets— some Japanese, some Chinese, some Hebrew (or any other alphabets).
- Stick them to the cards.
- Turn them face down on the table and you each take turns turning over and guessing what letter or word they represent.

Numbers

BE IT

VERSION 1

- Print out the face of a digital calculator.
- Stick it onto a poster board.
- Get some string and attach a loop to the top of the poster board so that it can go over your head.
- You have become a human calculator.

VERSION 2

- Take a number, any number. For example, let's take the number 7. Print out (or draw by hand) a row of seven emoji symbols. It could be:
  - the heart symbol
  - the cat symbol
  - flower symbols
  - any other emoji symbols that you think your child/ adult would really like.
- Make sure there are the same number of each symbol.
- Cut out each row of emojis and stick them somewhere on your face and body.

VERSION 3

- Draw the number 1 on your forehead with a face paint. Then put your arms straight up over your head so that you become the shape of number 1.
- Rub off the number 1 and face paint the number 2 on your forehead and make your body as best you can into the number 2.
- Keep doing this until you get to a number as high as you can. Of course, some numbers may be more than a little tricky, but it is the effort that counts here. Use your fingers, hands and feet. Have fun doing the best to make the number shape.

Abracadabra! Three different ways to become a human number.

Things you can do once you have become a number or calculator

For Version 1

- Start pressing the different numbers on the calculator and saying the numbers out loud.
- You can press math sums and say them out loud in different fun character voices (like Mickey Mouse) or animal sound effects. For example, 2+2 = 4.
- When you say the sum out loud you can add a bodily action. For example, say 2 sneezes plus 2 sneezes = 4 sneezes, then proceed to sneeze out loud. Then do another math sum in the same way. You could do the same and use:
    - pretend hiccups
    - burps
    - raspberries
    - pig snorts
    - duck quacks
    - sizzling sausage sounds
    - tickles
    - jumps
    - anything that motivates your child/adult.

- Press the longest number you can think of on your calculator, such as one trillion billion. That's a whole bunch of zeros!

For Version 2

- Point to the emojis on your body, such as the heart symbols, and count them. Then point to another set of emojis and count those.
- As you point to different symbols, sing this song to the tune of "Ten green bottles":
    There are seven red hearts just sitting on my tummy,
    Seven red hearts just sitting on my tummy.
    Then when seven red hearts accidentally fell,
    They all fell onto my right foot's toes.
- When you sing the last line, pull the seven heart emojis off you and stick them on the toes of your right foot.
- Make up as many verses to this song as you have pictures.
- Draw another symbol and put it on your body while your child/ adult is watching you.

For Version 3

When you physically become the number, do something fun. You could:
- jump up and down that many times
- sing how much you like being the number 1
- explode by making explosive sounds
- say, "Abracadabra" and become another number.

Things you could invite your child/adult to do
For Version 1

- Press the numbers on your calculator.
- Tell you what numbers to press.
- Tell you a sum to figure out on your human calculator.
- Write down a sum for you to figure out.
- Watch you press the numbers.
- Sneeze, or quack or jump with you.

For Version 2

- Pull an emoji row off your body.
- Find a certain emoji row on your body.
- Chase you and pull a row of emojis off.
- Draw a row of emojis and stick it on you.
- Tell you which emoji row they want.
- Stick rows on themselves.
- Count all the emoji rows to check they are all the same.
- Point to each emoji row.

For Version 3

- Draw a number on your forehead.
- Draw it on their forehead.
- Help you become the number 12. They make their body into a number 1 shape and you become the number 2.
- Sing with you.
- Watch you become each number.
- Tell you which number to draw on your forehead and try to be.

MAKE IT/DRAW IT

NUMBER PLATE GAME

- Get a bunch of cheap paper plates—around 20 of them.
- Excitedly take them out and write a number on each plate, 1–20.
- Once you have written a number on the plate, toss it on the floor. The number does not have to fall in order on the floor. Toss them here, there and everywhere.

Things you can do with the number plates

- Jump on all the prime numbers.
- Hop onto number 1, then say, "Where is number 2?" Then jump

to 2, then say, "Where is number 3?" and then hop to 3, until you have done all the numbers.

- Say the 2 times table while stepping on the plates with 2, 4, 6, 8 and so on.
- Get a ball and say, "I am going to make this land on number 7." Shout out another number and throw the ball onto that number plate. Keep going with all the numbers.
- Draw one object on the number 1 plate, two objects on the number 2 plate and so forth for all the numbers.
- Pick up all the plates and throw them into the air like unidentified flying saucers.
- Try anything else you can think of.

Things you could invite your child/adult to do

- Tell you what number to write on the plate.
- Throw a number plate onto the floor.
- Watch you write the numbers.
- Help you write the numbers on the plates.
- Jump or hop on the numbers with you.
- Jump on each number you call out.
- Tell you which number to jump or hop on.
- Point to where each number is so that you can jump onto them.
- Make each plate fly in the air like a Frisbee.
- Watch you throwing the plates in the air like a Frisbee.
- Play Frisbee with you with the plates.

NUMBER TOWER CRASH GAME

- Take any blocks or Lego bricks that you already have. It does not matter what size or shape they are.
- Tape a number to them. Or you can use the little circle stickers you can get cheaply from any stationery store and write a number in the circle and then stick it onto the blocks or bricks.
- Build a tower in numerical order, looking for the correct number to build with.

- When it gets to a certain number of your choice, make a figurine say loudly, "No tower in my town can be more than ten blocks high." Make the figurine drive a car into the tower to knock it down.
- Keep trying to rebuild past the number you are not supposed to build past. How far do you get before the figurine decides to knock it down? The game is to see how high you can build the tower before the figurine crashes it down.

Things you could invite your child/adult to do

- Watch you build the tower and crash it down.
- Build the number tower themselves.
- Be the one who gets the figurine to crash down the tower.
- Tell you how high to build the tower before the figurine comes to crash it down.
- Be the voice of the figurine.

MAKE A HUMAN NUMBER BOOK

- Print out seven pictures of your own face and seven pictures of your child/adult's face.
- On one page, write a big number 1 and an arrow to your nose.
- On another page, write a big number 1 and point an arrow to your tongue.
- On another page, write a big number 2 and an arrow to your eyes.
- Write another big number 1 and an arrow to your mouth.
- Write a big number 28 and draw an arrow to your teeth.
- On another page, write a big number 2 and draw an arrow to your nostrils.
- On another page, write a big number 2 and draw an arrow to your ears.

- You can do the same with any other facial feature you have, freckles, beauty marks and so on.
- Do the same with your child/adult's face. Or leave those pages blank for you and your child/adult to fill in together.
- Variation: Don't forget you can do the same idea with any body part. Or you can use pictures of animals or superheroes instead.

Things you could invite your child/adult to do

- Listen and look at the book and your face while you read it and point to your own face.
- Just look at the book.
- Point and count the facial features with you.
- Write the numbers and arrows in on their own blank faces.
- Point to your eyes and ears and so on.
- Point to their own eyes and ears and so on.

SHOWTIME IT

ROCKET LAUNCH GAME

- Take anything you can make into a rocket. It could be an actual toy rocket if you have one, or a picture of a rocket that you print out and stick on a piece of cardboard. Or it could just be a plain block that you are pretending is a rocket.
- The game is all about the suspenseful countdown to blast off.
- Count down from 10 to 1—each time you say a number spin around, jump up or put your arms in the air for a bit of dramatic anticipatory fun.
- Then of course at the end, catapult the rocket into space.
- Repeat.
- To make the fun go longer you can introduce a longer countdown of 20–1, or even 100–1.

Things you could invite your child/adult to do

- Count down with you.
- Watch you count and jump around.
- Watch you blast the rocket off.
- Blast the rocket into space themselves.
- Jump with you.
- Tell you how long to make the next countdown.

THE PUPPET WHO SPAT OUT NUMBERS GAME

- Use any puppet that you already have.
- Get some plastic numbers or number cards (anything that you already have).
- Put a number inside the mouth of your puppet.
- Have the puppet spit the numbers out in fun ways all over the room.

Things you could invite your child/adult to do

- Watch you make the puppet spit out numbers.
- Pick up the numbers and give them to you.
- Put the number in the puppet's mouth.
- Tell the puppet which number to spit out.
- Put a puppet on their own hand and have it spit out a number.

SING NUMBER SONGS

- Here are some links to some number songs:
  - This one has a whole bunch for the under-fives: https://youtu.be/V_lgJgBbqWE
  - Here are some for the over-fives: https://youtu.be/zmvvhV1MrOk
- Hold up the numbers or draw them as you sing.

Note: These are for you to watch and learn the songs to sing to your child/adult, not for your child/adult to watch.

Things you could invite your child/adult to do

- Watch you as you sing to them.
- Dance as you sing.
- Do the actions with you.
- Sing along.
- Hold the number you are singing about.
- Tell you which song to sing.

SUPERFACT IT

RESEARCH INTERESTING FACTS ABOUT NUMBERS

Find out about anything you can think of that your child/adult will be interested in. Here are some topics to inspire your research:

- Famous mathematicians, what did they discover or learn about to make them famous?
- The history of the calculator.
- How was the abacus used?
- Is the abacus the oldest calculator?
- How music is really math.
- What is calculus?
- How does a mathematician figure out the speed of light?
- What equation has never been solved and what would it solve if it was?
- Who is the youngest mathematician of note who is alive today?
- These are some of the toughest equations ever solved. Learn what you can about them:
  - The Collatz Conjecture—Dave Linkletter
  - Goldbach's Conjecture
  - The Twin Prime Conjecture
  - The Riemann Hypothesis
  - The Birch and Swinnerton-Dyer Conjecture
  - The Kissing Number Problem

- The Unknotting Problem
- The Large Cardinal Project.
- These are interesting number sequences. What are these numbers?
  - Odd numbers
  - Even numbers
  - Prime numbers
  - Square numbers
  - Triangular numbers
  - Fibonacci sequence.
- Codes: What is the first number code to be invented. Who invented it?
- What is a mathmagician?

How you can use this information with your child/adult

Share it with your child/adult

- Have a discussion together about all the interesting facts.
- Ask them what other information and facts they would be curious to know about numbers.
- As you talk, write out the numbers or the equations or show them printouts of them.
- Share your thoughts and opinions on the information you found. Do you think it is interesting? Do you understand it; what is difficult or easy for you about the different numbers?

Name that Number Game

- Put number names/sequences on a piece of paper. For example:
  - Prime number
  - Odd number
  - Even number
  - Square number
  - Triangular number
  - Fibonacci sequence.
- Fold the paper over so no one can see what it is and put all the pieces in a bowl.

- When you pick out a piece of paper, you have to say numbers that represent the number name or sequence on the paper.
- The other person gets to agree or challenge you. If they challenge you, they have to say which number is incorrect and what a correct number would be.
- A variation would be to put numbers on the pieces of paper in a bowl, and you have to say what sequence these numbers belong to. To get higher numbers, you could pick out two or three numbers at the same time from the bowl.

Number debate

- You each decide what number or number sequence you like best. Is it all numbers with a 7 in? Is it prime numbers? Is it a particular equation?
- You each create a list of reasons why yours is the best. They could include:
  - why you like the number
  - why this number is useful for the world
  - what about it makes it beautiful
  - what you can do with this number.
- You are going to hold a debate called "Which number is best?"
- Create two "podiums" where each person talks from.
- You could write out invitations for family members to attend the debate.
- The audience gets to pick who they agree with most.
- Tally up the votes.
- Other topics you could debate are:
  - Which mathematician contributed the most to society and why?
  - Is math or art more important for world peace?

Household Appliances

All of these games can be applied to any household appliances. Use whichever one your child/adult is really into. For example, if the game talks about vacuum cleaners and your child/adult is into blenders, do the exact same thing, but use a blender instead.

BE IT

These examples are all for making yourself become a washing machine.

VERSION 1

- Get a giant box (see the "Materials" section in Chapter 3 to know how to get your hands on one of these).
- Open the top and the bottom so it becomes a tunnel and cut a round hole in the middle of each of the sides so that your arms can come through it.
- Draw a few control buttons on the box—On/Off buttons, a dial for the different kinds of cycles (extra spin, delicate spin, economy wash and so on—just use the ones that are on your own washing machine).
- Cut a big circular flap in the front of the box so that it can be a door that opens and closes.
- Climb inside it and put your arms through the holes in the side, and away you go! You are a human washing machine!

VERSION 2

- Get two big plastic bags or bin liners.
- Attach them to your chest and back (safety pins or masking tape work well for this). The bags are for you to load the clothes into.
- With clear sticky tape, stick an On/Off button to your shirt, just above the bags.
- Stick on a dial that shows the different kinds of cycles—again just use the ones that are on your own washing machine.

VERSION 3

- Get a poster board and draw a big square washing machine shape on the front with the words "washing machine."
- Draw the On/Off button and a dial with the different kinds of cycles.
- Attach a plastic bag to the back of the poster board (for the clothes to go into).
- Get some string and attach a loop to the top of the poster board so that it can go over your head.

Abracadabra! You have three different ways to become a human washing machine.

Things you can do once you have become a washing machine

- Have a pile of clothes and put them one by one into your washing machine in a lively and entertaining way:
  - Push the On button.
  - Make silly washing machine sound effects.
  - Shake like a washing machine might.
- Draw a bunch of paper clothes together with your child/adult and put them into the washing machine (i.e., you).

- Say you are hungry as you have no more clothes to put in and chase your child/adult, trying to catch them so that you can put one of their socks into the machine.
- Put the washing machine on different spin cycles and spin or shake in fun and different ways. For example:
  - The extra spin cycle is fast.
  - The delicate cycle is slow and wavy; you could dance with your arms in the air like a ballerina.
  - The economy cycle is bumpy.
- Pick up your child and give them different kinds of washing machine rides depending on the cycle you or they choose.
- Put as many clothes in the washing machine as possible, press the On button, and then start spinning around faster and faster. Announce that the washing machine is out of control and won't stop, and then make the clothes explode and fly all across the room.

Things you could invite your child/adult to do

- Press the buttons.
- Say the words "on," "off," "spin," "cycle," "delicate cycle," "extra spin cycle."
- Pick up the clothes and put them in the machine.
- Draw clothes for the washing machine.
- Ride on the washing machine.
- Tell you which piece of clothing to put in the washing machine.
- Dress up like a washing machine themselves.

MAKE IT/DRAW IT

BUILD A "TOWN OF BLENDERS"

- You can use any kind of blocks you have in the house, or any cardboard boxes that you have saved.
- The town has three streets.
- Instead of houses, on each street there are different blender appliances (each block or cardboard box represents a blender).

- Each brand has its own street, such as:
  - Breville Street
  - Nutribullet Avenue
  - Kitchen Aid Road.

Things you could invite your child/adult to do

- Build the town with you.
- Name the streets.
- Roll cars down the roads.
- Roll delivery trucks down the road with different pretend food items to leave at the doorstep of each blender "house."
- Watch you build it and roll cars down the streets.

MAKE THE FURNITURE INTO AN APPLIANCE

- A chair can be a vacuum cleaner:
  - Attach a plastic bag to the back of the chair (for all the rubbish it will pick up).
  - Push it along the floor making a vacuum sound.
- Lay crunched up paper and food wrappers on the floor.
- Push the chair along the floor. It "eats" up the paper (i.e., you pick it up and put it in the plastic bag you attached to the chair).
- Alternatively, you could use a little table turned upside-down, or a broom as the vacuum cleaner.

Things you could invite your child/adult to do

- Put out the rubbish for the vacuum to pick up.
- Tell you where to push the cleaner.
- Push the cleaner themselves.
- Make their own vacuum with another chair:
  - Race with you to see who can pick up the most rubbish.
  - Say the word "on" and "off" to make the cleaner go and stop.
  - Make the sound effects for the vacuum.
- Watch you do the vacuuming.

VACUUM STORY BOOK

- Get a story book that is at the age of your child/adult and recreate it using a vacuum as the hero of the story. For example, instead of *The Tiger Who Came to Tea* you would read the story as *The Vacuum Who Came to Tea*. Just swop out any mention of the word tiger and use the vacuum instead. Now you have loads of vacuum stories at your fingertips.

Other things you can do with the vacuum story book

- Get a poster board and stick it up on a wall.
- Start drawing a vacuum cleaner. It doesn't have to be great; you can draw a "stick-like vacuum" similar to how you would draw a "stick man."
- Draw the story out on the poster board.
- You could also draw the story on a chalk board or a whiteboard.
- Act out the story using a toy vacuum, or your real vacuum.

Things you could invite your child/adult to do

- Turn the pages in the book.
- Listen to you reading the story.
- Say the word "vacuum" instead of the main character of the story.
- Draw part of the story on the whiteboard or chalk board.
- Make up a new part of the story.
- Read you the story.
- Sit next to you while you read.

SHOWTIME IT

TOILET CATALOG GAME

- Get a toilet catalog. (You can order one online.) If possible, get a Japanese catalog, as they have more interesting and advanced toilets.
- Show your child/adult the catalog.
- Read out loud to them about the different features of the various models.
- Read out loud the different prices for the toilets.
- Make the flushing sounds that you think each toilet would have.

Things you could invite your child/adult to do

- Turn the pages.
- Sit beside you and just look at the catalog.
- Point to the one they like the best.
- Name the one they like the best.

TOILET PUPPET SHOW

- Cut out pictures of two different toilets.
- Stick them onto a long stick (or wooden spoon).
- Draw faces on the lids of the toilets to personalize them.
- You have made two toilet puppets.
- Put on a puppet show where:
  - the two toilets meet and fall in love
  - the toilets are both looking for their long-lost cousin, Ben the Bidet. They go on an adventure to find him. They look all through the whole of their own country. No luck. Then they go to Africa by boat or by plane. No luck there. They eventually find him on a sheep farm in Australia. Or make up any story you want.

Things you could invite your child/adult to do

- Watch you do the puppet show.
- Clap at the end of the show.
- Hold one of the toilet puppets and move it about.
- Be the voice of one of the toilet puppets.
- Help you make the toilet puppets.

SONGS ABOUT APPLIANCES

- Make up a rhyme about your child/adult's favorite appliance. Make it really cheesy. For inspiration, here's one about a blender:

    Ooh, how I love my blender
    It makes me oh so slender
    Just throw in a strawberry, cinnamon and a cherry
    I drink it and then become very merry
    It twirls, it whirls, just like my curls
    Oh, give me a blender
    And I will show you its splendor.

- Add a verse about their favorite appliance to the song "If you're happy and you know it..." that says, for example, "...sound like a washing machine," or "...run round like a vacuum," or "...beep like a microwave." And, of course, add in any actions you can.
- Add a verse about their favorite appliance to the nursery rhyme "Old MacDonald Had a Farm" that says, for example, "and on that farm...
    - he had a blender"—then make blender sound effects
    - he had a toilet"—then make toilet sound effects
    - he had a microwave"—then make microwave sound effects.
- Take any current popular song and see how many times you can put the word "washing machine" or different makes and models of blenders or vacuum cleaners into the lyrics.

SUPERFACT IT

RESEARCH INTERESTING FACTS ABOUT YOUR CHILD/ADULT'S FAVORITE APPLIANCE

Here are some topics to inspire your research:

- Who invented it?
- Find a picture of the first one ever created.
- How fast, heavy and efficient was it?
- How much did one cost?
- How was it developed?
- What was it first used for?
- What is it used for now?
- How many uses does it have?
- Find as many facts as you can about the current different makes and models and prices:
  - Which one is considered the best?
  - What make has the most range?
  - How are they rated by online buyers (i.e., which is rated the worst and the best)?
  - How many of these appliances would an average person own over a lifetime?
  - What is the average life span of this appliance?
  - Any other information you can find.

How you can use this information with your child/adult

Share it with your child/adult

- Have a discussion together about it.
- Ask them what other information and facts they would be curious to know about an appliance.
- As you talk, show them pictures of the appliance you are talking about. Read out quotes or sections from articles you've found. Show them the blueprints of the controls. Show them blueprints of any engine they use, and user manuals.
- Share your thoughts and opinions on the information you found.

Do you think it is interesting? If money was no issue, what make and model of the appliance would you buy?

- What appliance would you invent or want to see on the market?

Make a quiz show

- With the information you gather, create 20 questions about the appliance of choice.
- Have fun seeing how many answers you each know.
- Don't forget to help each other out. You get extra points for helping the other person.

Make an appliance board game

- Draw 20 squares on a poster board in the shape of an "S."
- Number each square.
- Stick a picture of your child/adult's favorite appliance on every fourth square.
- Use just one dice.
- Create "appliance cards." Depending on the level of your child/ adult, each appliance card could have:
  - a picture of a different appliance on it that they get to keep
  - a question on it about something to do with the appliance. If they answer correctly, they get to keep the card
  - a fun fact on it about the appliance
  - an action to do. It could be to make the appliance's sound effect, or pretend they are the appliance.
- If you land on a square with a picture of an appliance you pick up an "appliance card."
- Keep going around the board until all the cards are used up.

Vehicles

BE IT

Become your child/adult's favorite vehicle.

VERSION 1

- Print out a license plate number and a car emblem.
- Get a sheet, sari or blanket.
- Tape the car emblem to your forehead and the license plate number to the blanket.
- Hold onto the blanket and move around making car sounds.
- What a great car you have become!

VERSION 2

- Create a helicopter hat.
- Take a poster board and cut two long strips approximately 5 inches wide.
- With masking tape, tape them to a baseball hat (or any other hat you have).
- Wear it. Declare you are a helicopter, and then move the hat around in a circle on your head and jump up pretending you are flying.
- You are a helicopter!

VERSION 3

> • Make the sound effect of your child/adult's favorite vehicle and move around the room like a car, train, plane or horse and cart.

Abracadabra! Three different ways to become a vehicle.

Things you can do once you have become this vehicle

- Go over to different stuffed animals or figurines and invite them to board your vehicle. Then drive, fly or push/pull them around the room.
- Pretend to crash into the wall, or mountain if you are a plane, or sink in the sea if you are a boat.
- Slow down and speed up, go left, right, forwards, backwards or in a circle. Drive on or under the furniture.
- Consult your GPS for directions. You can pretend to use the touch screen (which is really the air) or verbally ask the (pretend) GPS for directions and then make it answer with a fun robotic accent. Then follow the GPS directions. Use your imagination and humor and have your GPS send you to differ-ent places. For example:
  - to the kitchen to get some food
  - to the teddy bear's belly button for a tickle
  - up the nostril of the puppet (ooh—what will you find there?)
  - to the bottom of the sea to get some treasure
  - to the store to pick a new book to read. Once you are at the bookstore, you could read a story.

  Nothing is off limits; go with the first idea that comes into your head.
- Dress up as a pilot, a ship's captain, pirate, or Nascar racer.

Things you could invite your child/adult to do

- Verbally tell you where to go to.
- Use gestures to indicate where the vehicle should go.
- Get on board (i.e., sit on your back, or on your lap, and take a ride in your human vehicle).

- Put the soft animals or figurines into the "vehicle."
- Become the voice of the GPS.
- Press the pretend buttons on the GPS.
- Become the vehicle themselves.
- Create a mountain out of blocks for you to crash into.

MAKE IT/DRAW IT

SPAGHETTI JUNCTION GAME

- Create intertwining roads on the floor with artist tape.
- Create a tunnel out of a cardboard box. You can do this by getting any box and cutting an archway for your child/adult's toy vehicle to go through on either side of the box.
- Have fun driving your cars along the roads.

Things you could do once you have made the roads and tunnel

- Create a high-speed police car chase.
- Rush a vet ambulance to a stuffed bear who has been involved in a hit-and-run accident.
- The tunnel is magic; when a car goes through it transforms into a flying car.
- Create destinations by putting pictures at the end of each road. They could be pictures of:
  - a park
  - a supermarket
  - a school
  - Aladdin's cave
  - anything that would interest your child/adult.

Things you could invite your child/adult to do

- Watch as you make the roads.

- Help you make the roads.
- Hand you the artist tape to make the roads.
- Tell you how to make the roads.
- Cut the tunnel with you.
- Roll the cars along the roads.
- Roll a car in the high-speed chase.
- Choose which road to take to what destination.
- Be the vet who helps the stuffed bear involved in the hit-and-run.

HELIPORT REFUELING STATION

- Mark an "H" on the floor with artist tape. The "H" indicates where the helicopter is to land.
- Make two flags to wave to guide the helicopter into the heliport.
- Take turns being the person who waves the flags so that the helicopter can land and fills the helicopter up again with fuel. Or the pilot of the helicopter flying in to land at the heliport.
- The helicopter could be you or your child/adult pretending that they are a helicopter or an actual helicopter toy, or a picture of a helicopter.

Things you could invite your child/adult to do

- Fly the helicopter to land on top of the "H."
- Ask you (aka the mechanic) to mend the engine or refuel.
- Be the mechanic and fix your helicopter or refuel it for you.
- Watch you fly the helicopter onto the "H."
- Tape the "H" on the floor in different places for the helicopter to land.
- Wave the flags so that you can see where to land your helicopter.
- Put on the pilot hat.
- Hold a toy tool.
- Pretend to fix the engine with a toy spanner or other tool.

AIRPLANE BOARDING GAME

- Get 12 pieces of paper and write "boarding pass" on each one.
- Get another 12 pieces of A4 paper and write an airplane seat number on each piece of paper. The seat numbers could be as follows: 1A, 1B, 1C, 1D, 2A, 2B, 2C, 2D, 3A, 3B, 3C, 3D.
- Lay out the pieces of paper on the floor in three rows of four with an aisle down the middle, like airplane seats would be arranged.
- Cut two long pieces of string.
- Make a curved shape with the string to indicate the nose of the plane, and a tail shape with the string to indicate the end of the airplane.
- Abracadabra! You just made a big plane!
- Now the plane is ready for boarding.
- Get ten stuffed animals or figurines and put them in the "gate" area to the side of the plane. They are waiting to board the plane.
- Give out the boarding passes to everyone.
- Call each person in to board one by one.
- Seat everyone in their correct place.
- Fly somewhere, land and repeat with more passengers.

Things you could invite your child/adult to do

- Help you make the plane.
- Help each passenger into their seat.
- Sit on one of the airplane "seats" themselves.
- Watch you seat everyone.
- Step into the airplane.
- Hand out the boarding passes.
- Call everyone in by seat number to board the plane.
- Choose who the passengers are going to be.
- Make seatbelts for everyone.
- Act out the usual safety announcement before take-off.
- Put signs up for the exits.

SHOWTIME IT

ALL ABOARD GAME

- Wear a cap with "Train Conductor" written or stuck on it.
- Wear a black coat or jumper to make yourself look more like a train conductor.
- Put on a name tag: "Frank—Train Conductor." You can use any name you like.
- Have a whistle to blow—or whistle yourself if you can.
- Get three pieces of paper and write "Train Station" on each one.
- Place the pieces of paper in different parts of the room.
- Place three figurines on each of the paper station platforms.
- Get some toy trains (or pictures of trains) and roll them into the first station. Before it gets to the first station yell out, "The seaside train is approaching Platform One. Please stand back from the platform."
- Drive the train into the station.
- Call out, "All aboard, all aboard the seaside train!"
- Once everyone is aboard blow the whistle to inform the driver it is time to leave the station.
- Repeat the above steps with the other two stations.
- Put the passengers back on the platforms and repeat for as long as your child/adult is interested.

Things you could invite your child/adult to do

- Roll the train into the stations.
- Write "Train Station" on the pieces of paper.
- Watch you roll the train into the stations and board the people.
- Call out "All aboard, all aboard!"
- Help the passengers onto the train.
- Give you the thumbs-up when all the passengers have boarded the train and it is okay for you to roll the train out of the station.

- Blow the whistle so that the driver knows it is safe to leave the station.
- Make the noise of the train.

GARBAGE PICK UP DAY GAME

- Get three buckets. They are going to become trash cans.
- Label one "Paper," one "Trash" and one "Plastic."
- Collect your own real recycling cardboard and plastic items and use some dead flowers or apple cores, used tissues or banana peel as the real trash. Mix it up into one garage bag. Place by the three bucket bins.
- The phone rings (you make the ringing sound).
- You pick it up (using your hands as the phone).
- Listen intently, then shout out, "It's garbage collection day; the garbage trucks are coming. Must sort the garbage."
- Then sort through it putting all the items in the correct bucket in a fun and silly way.
- Once done, shout out, "I hear the trucks, here they come."
- Then push a laundry basket over or a big cardboard box. These can be the garbage truck. If you have a toy truck, you could use that.
- Dump the trash in the truck. With the toy truck, you won't get much in it, but that is okay—you can come back for more.
- As you load the trucks with garbage don't forget to make the beeping sounds and noise of the real garbage trucks.
- Drive it away to the dump—which is somewhere in the same room.
- Dump it out.
- Drive back for the plastic.
- Drive to the dump.
- Drive back for the paper.
- Drive to the dump.

Things you could invite your child/adult to do

- Watch you pick up the trash.
- Help you sort the trash into the correct bucket bins.
- Put some trash in the garbage trucks.
- Dump the trash out in the correct place at the dump.
- Tell you when the garbage truck is full and ready to go to the dump.
- Tell you when it has been unloaded and is ready to get some more.
- Make the sound effects with you.
- Help you collect the trash for the game.

DEMOLITION DERBY

- Get all the vehicles you have.
- It's a free for all.
- Cars are driving everywhere.
- Trucks are doing wheelies.
- Airplanes are flying over cars.
- Vehicles are racing each other.
- All the vehicles are crashing into one another.
- In other words, drive them, crash them, fly them all over the room in crazy, interesting ways.
- Keep doing this for as long as your child/adult is interested.

Things you could invite your child/adult to do

- Watch you.
- Join in.
- Come up with crazy car stunts.

SUPERFACT IT

RESEARCH INTERESTING FACTS ABOUT VEHICLES

Specifically, find out about the particular vehicle that your child/adult likes. Here are some topics to inspire your research:

- The most expensive cars in the world.
- The smallest vehicles in the world.
- The fastest car in the world.
- Racing tracks of the world. It could be rally race driving, the Grand Prix, horse and carriage racing competitions, demolition derbies.
- Army vehicles.
- How the engine of a car, helicopter or airplane works.
- The controls of an airplane, the steps you have to follow to take off and land.
- The most famous helicopter crashes of all time.
- Lorries—all the different kinds, and the different gears they have. What kind of cargo do they carry and how do they store it?
- The history of the hovercraft.
- The *Titanic.*
- The oldest shipwrecks found around the world.
- Driverless cars.
- Different license plates in different countries.

How to use this information with your child/adult

Share it with your child/adult

- Have a discussion together about all the information you find.
- Ask them what other information and facts they would be curious to know about any vehicle.
- As you talk, show them pictures of the vehicles you are talking about. Show them the blueprints of the controls in an airplane or helicopter. Show them blueprints of an engine.
- Share your thoughts and opinions on the information you found.

Do you think it is interesting? If money was no issue, and you had three vehicles, what would they be? Would you be comfortable riding in a driverless car?

Make your own personalized license plate

- Give your child/adult a piece of paper and markers.
- They come up with their license plate without seeing yours.
- You come up with yours without seeing theirs.
- Then show each other your license plates.
- Guess why each of you chose the numbers and letters you did.
- What personal significance do they have?
- Variation: Design what your child/adult's vehicle of choice would look like if it was made in 2060:
  - What cool futuristic features would it have?
  - What would it look like?
  - How would it move?
  - How would the engine work?
  - What would the interior look like?

Books

BE IT

VERSION 1

- Photocopy your child/adult's favorite book.
- Staple all the pages together in one corner, so that it is easy to tear a page off to reveal the next page.
- Safety pin it to your shirt.

VERSION 2

- Get a big poster board and fold it in half so that it is just like the cover of a book.
- Write the name of one of your child/adult's favorite books on the front.
- Stand inside it and hold it under one of your armpits so you can open and close the "book" with the other hand.

VERSION 3

- Tape blank pieces of paper to yourself—on your chest, down your legs and arms.
- You are a blank manuscript ready to be written on.

Abracadabra! Three different ways to become a human book.

Things you can do once you have become a book

For Version 1

- Start reading the story using an excited and energetic, fun voice.
- After reading a page, tear it off and do something interesting with it, such as:
  - Scrunch it up into a ball and throw it in a basketball hoop.
  - Roll it up and make it into a telescope.
  - Fold it into a paper airplane and fly it across the room.

For Version 2

- Pop out of the book in fun and interesting ways.
- Each time you open the book, say two lines of the story. Close the book, open it again and say another two lines of the story. And so forth.
- Get some small objects that are relevant to the book story and put them in your pockets. Once inside the book, take an object out and open the book to reveal the object. Close it again and take out another object. Open the book to reveal it. (*The objects could be little like a sticker, or a letter, or a figurine.*)

For Version 3

- Get a pen and start writing the story on the blank pages. Read it quietly to yourself and then laugh. Get a different colored pen and write on another piece of paper. Keep going.
- Draw story cartoon pictures of stick figures having a conversation with each other in speech bubbles. They could be telling each other silly "knock-knock" jokes. These are easy to find on the internet.
- Say your story out loud as you write it.
- Write the story of a book or movie you know your child/adult likes on the blank pages.

Things you could invite your child/adult to do

For Version 1

- Tear off a page of the book so you can read the next page.
- Make the torn-off page into something like a ball or a plane.
- Tell you to read.
- Look at the book as you read it.
- Look at you as you read the story.

For Version 2

- Take the toy you have hiding in the big poster board book.
- Open the book.
- Ask you to say the next two lines in the story book.
- Get in the book themselves.
- Pop out of the book themselves.
- Tell you to pop out.
- Watch you pop out of the book.

For Version 3

- Come up with part of the story you are writing.
- Sing with you.
- Write on one of your pages.
- Write a joke in your cartoon story.
- Draw a picture in your book.
- Stick paper on themselves and write their own book.

MAKE IT/DRAW IT

MISHMASH BOOK

- Photocopy one page from ten of your child/adult's favorite books.
- Put all the pages together.
- Hole punch down on one side.

- Tie them together into a book.
- It's the mishmash book.
- Don't forget to laugh when you read the funny mishmash book.

Things you could invite your child/adult to do

- Listen to the mishmash story.
- Watch you read it to them.
- Guess which book each page comes from.
- Make their own mishmash book.
- Guess which page from which book is coming next.
- Turn the pages.

SILLY FACE BOOK

- Take a picture of each family member making a silly face.
- Print the photos out.
- Stick each photo onto a different sheet of paper.
- Make it into a book.

Things you could invite your child/adult to do

- Make a new silly expression and take a photo for the silly face book.
- Turn the pages in the book.
- Read the book with you.
- Make the expressions in the book.
- Look at the book.
- Listen to you reading the book.
- Make the book with you. They could:
  - hole punch the pages
  - tie the pages together.

PHOTO BOOK

- Take a picture of your child/adult:
  - eating
  - sleeping
  - sitting on the potty
  - walking
  - jumping
  - running
  - reading
  - doing anything you decide.
- Print the photos out.
- Stick each photo onto a different sheet of paper.
- Make it into a book.

Things you could invite your child/adult to do

- Act out what they are doing in the photos.
- Name what they are doing in the photos.
- Point to themselves in the photos.
- Look at you while you read the book.
- Look at the book with you.
- Turn the pages.
- Pose doing something new for the photo book.

SHOWTIME IT

CIRCLE FACE BOOK SHOW

- Take six pieces of colored card. Each piece of card needs to be big enough to cover your whole face. Regular copy paper or A4 or legal size colored card would work well.
- Cut out a circle in the middle of each card. Make the circle big enough so that when you put it up to your face your whole face will show.
- Put all the pieces of card with the cut-out circle together.

- Hole punch the top of each card.
- Tie them together to make a book that you can open and turn the page at the top instead of at the side.
- Next, cut out pictures of different hats:
  - A crown
  - A builder's hat
  - A fireman's hat
  - A policeman's hat
  - A tiara
  - Any other hat you can think of.
- Get a bunch of stickers—any shape or color.

How to do the show

- Put the book up to your face so that your face is peeking through. Make sure that the hole-punch part is at the top (above your forehead). Then do one of the following things.
  - Make a silly face—such as stick your tongue out.
    » Turn the page. Remember the page turns at the top of the book, so when you turn it that page will rest on the top of your head and your face will show on a different colored card ready for a new expression.
    » Keep making different silly faces until the book is finished.
  - Put a sticker on your face.
    » Turn the page. Remember the page turns at the top of the book, so when you turn it that page will rest on the top of your head and your face will show on a different colored card ready for a new sticker.
    » Keep putting on another sticker until the book is finished.
  - Stick one of the hat pictures on the top of the circle, so it looks as if you are wearing a hat.
  - Turn the page. Remember the page turns at the top of the book, so when you turn it that page will rest on the top of your head and your face will show on a different colored card ready to stick a new hat on the top of the circle.
  - Keep sticking on different hats until the book is finished.

Things you could invite your child/adult to do

- Turn the pages.
- Watch you do all the activities with the book.
- Do a silly face with you too.
- Tell you what type of silly face to do.
- Put a sticker on your face.
- Put a sticker on their own face.
- Tell you which sticker to use and where to put it.
- Put a hat on your "head."
- Tell you which hat to put on.
- Take a turn doing the circle face book themselves.

LIBRARY GAME

- Get 20+ of your child/adult's favorite books.
- Line up all the books in a row on a shelf. If you do not have a shelf, line them up on the floor so that they are standing up, leaning against the wall.
- Get a poster board or paper and write the words, "Welcome to the library." Stick it on the wall.
- Get a cardboard box, laundry basket, plastic bag or anything that you can use as a shopping basket.
- Put a stuffed animal in your "shopping basket." Push the stuffed animal around and have them point to different books they want. Put each book they choose in your "shopping basket."
- Pretend to drive home.
- Once home, read the books.
- When finished, pretend to drive back to the library. Return the books and choose some different ones.
- Drive home and read them.
- Repeat as many times as you want.

Things you could invite your child/adult to do

- Get in the "shopping basket."

- Point to the books they want.
- Put the books they want into the "shopping basket."
- Listen to the books you chose.
- Read the books they chose to you.
- Pretend to drive the car.
- Turn the pages in the book.
- Put the books back on the shelf or lined up against the wall.
- Rearrange the books in the library.
- Choose which books to put in the library.

STORY BOOK SCENE GAME

- Make a page of your child/adult's favorite book come alive by recreating the illustration from that page as best you can.
- If it is an alphabet book, you could put a plastic letter "A" with an apple beside it.
- If it is *Goldilocks and the Three Bears*, you could create the page where Goldilocks is sleeping in one of the three beds.
- It might be a book about Mickey Mouse. Let's say the page your child/adult likes the best is where Mickey Mouse is driving in a car with Minnie Mouse. Get a truck or car and put a Minnie and Mickey Mouse figurine in it (or pictures of both if you do not have their figurines). If there are other cars in the picture, place them where they are in the picture. Try to get it as similar as you can.

Things you can do once you have recreated the scene

- Show your child/adult the picture and then your scene.
- Add one more thing to the scene that you have left out.
- Turn the page and create the next scene.
- Say the storyline.
- Do another page, and so on.

- If your child/adult only has one favorite page in each book, just do that page for each book.
- Once the scene is set, move it to act out different parts of the storyline.

Things you could invite your child/adult to do

- Watch you make the scene.
- Help you make the scene.
- Show you the next page to recreate.
- Say the storyline.
- Move the scene to act out more of the story.

SUPERFACT IT

RESEARCH INTERESTING FACTS ABOUT BOOKS

Specifically, find out about the book or books your child/adult likes. Here are some topics to inspire your research:

- How many books has their favorite author written? What are their titles?
- Interesting facts about the life of their favorite author.
- The history of books themselves. How did they start? What is the oldest book?
- Where is the oldest book housed?
- How many books are sold on Amazon, each day or each year?
- How can you publish your own book?
- How old is the youngest author?
- Find out everything you can about the *Guinness Book of World Records*.
- What are the Akashic Records?
- How do you print a book?

How to use this information with your child/adult

Share it with your child/adult

- Have a discussion together about these interesting facts.
- Ask them what other information or facts they would be curious to know about books.
- As you talk, show them pictures of the books you are talking about. Read out quotes or sections from them.
- Share your own thoughts and opinions on the information you found. Do you think it is interesting? People say everyone has a book in them; what would be yours? Share your favorite book of all time and why.

Name that Book Title

- Write down different quotes from books that your child or adult has read, each on separate pieces of paper.
- Put them in a bowl.
- The game is for them to take one out and see if they can name the title of the book.
- How many books can they guess? If they can't guess, give them more clues about the plot and storyline, or the author.

Storyline Game

- Make a list of ten titles of books that you are sure your child/adult has not read, and that you have not read. These titles could come from the classics or be ten random fiction titles that you find on an internet search. The Penguin Classics website is great for inspiration, and it also gives a synopsis of each book.
- The game is to take turns making up what the storyline/plot is for that title.
- Once you have both come up with your individual storyline, read the actual story synopsis and see if either of you were close.

Maps, Road Signs, Traffic Lights and Subways

BE IT

VERSION 1

- Print out a bunch of road maps from the internet. Print enough pages to cover most if not all of you.
- Cut them so that only the map part is showing (i.e., cut out the advertisements and so on).
- Tape each page to your body so that it covers the whole of your front. (Don't do your back, because, if possible, you want your child/adult to be in front of you so that there are opportunities for you to look at each other.)

VERSION 2

- Print out different road signs, for example: a stop sign, a dead-end sign, 10 more miles to Route 22. Use your child/adult's favorite road signs.
- Tape a road sign to the underpart of each of your arms so that they are completely visible only when you lift your arms up.
- Put one on each of the soles of your feet and one on the palm of each hand.

- When your child/adult is looking at you, flash them a road sign and say the name of it in the voice of your GPS.
- Have a stack of other road signs with tape already on the back of them, so that you can quickly swop the road signs for new ones.

VERSION 3

- Get a big enough box so that you can get inside it, or use a laundry basket or a dustbin. Or make a den out of the furniture and a blanket and get inside it.
- Depending on what you are going to be, make a sign that reads something like: "Map Oracle" or "Road Signs Expert" or "Traffic Light Officer" or "Subway Directions Genius." (Be whichever one you think your child/adult might most like.)
- Have printed out maps if you are going to be a "Map Oracle", road signs if you are going to be a "Road Signs Expert", subway maps if you are going to be a "Subway Directions Genius", and "Go" and "Stop" signs if you are going to be a "Traffic Light Officer."
- Get in the box/den/laundry basket (if you get in a laundry basket put a blanket over you so you are totally hidden).
- Pop out of the box, basket or den and hold up the sign to tell your child/adult what you are. Introduce yourself.
- Pop back down into the box, den or laundry basket.
- Pop back out again with a map, road sign, subway map or "Go" or "Stop" sign. Hold it out so your child/adult can see it.
- Then pop back in and pop up with another. Continue.

Abracadabra! Three ways to become a map, a road sign or a traffic light.

Things you can do once you have become a map/road sign/traffic light

For Version 1

- Take a pen and draw a route out on one of the maps on your body.
- Roll a toy car along one of the maps.
- Say the different routes out loud, naming each junction and road number.
- Become the "Map Monster" and chase your child/adult

For Version 2

- Keep flashing different road signs to your child/adult.
- Say the names of the road signs as you show them.
- Sing the different road signs as you show them.
- Show them by doing different dance moves.
  - Do the "Can-Can" with your legs so that your child/adult can see the signs on your feet.
  - Do the chicken dance as you show the road signs that are underneath your arms.
- Keep switching to different signs to surprise them with a new sign.

For Version 3

- Pop out of the box/den, share the sign and say its meaning.
- Pop out of the box and declare, "I am here for any directions anyone might want," then pop down again.
- Pop up and say, "Knock three times if you want some directions."
- Pop up and give the route directions from your house to Grandma's house.
- Pop up and present a map. Point out the different destinations on the map.
- Pop up and declare that you are a traffic light. Have fun telling them to stop, go, walk/don't walk and so on.

Things you could invite your child/adult to do

For Version 1

- Draw a line following the route they like the best on your maps.
- Say the name of the roads on your maps.
- Count how many junctions are on your maps.
- Count how many roads are on your maps.
- Watch you as you point to different destinations on your maps.
- Stick maps on themselves.
- Roll cars along your maps.
- Pull the maps off you.

For Version 2

- Say, "sign," "map" or "show me X."
- Pretend to be in a car and when you hold up the sign they do whatever the sign tells them to, for example they stop driving when you show a stop sign.
- Tape a sign onto their own hands. You pretend to be driving in a car. They show you the sign on their hands and you respond according to the sign they show you, for example if it is a stop sign you stop the car.
- Look at you.
- Make different road signs to stick on you or them.

For Version 3

- Take the sign or map from you.
- Say the words "up" or "pop up" or "Help Mr Map Oracle" or "Are you open?" Or knock three times at your door.
- Pretend to ring a bell to get you to pop up.
- Take turns becoming the oracle, expert or officer themselves.
- Respond to you as a traffic light by stopping at red, going at green, getting ready at amber.

MAKE IT/DRAW IT

MAP PUZZLE GAME

- Take a map that your child/adult knows really well.
- Cut it up into ten squares.
- You have a map puzzle!
- Stick the puzzle pieces to you.
- Pull off a piece one at a time and put the puzzle together.

Things you could invite your child/adult to do

- Look at the puzzle pieces.
- Pull one off.
- Find the next puzzle piece that goes with the piece that you have already pulled off.
- Make a map puzzle themselves.
- Say, "puzzle" or "map."

TRAFFIC LIGHT DELIGHT GAME

- Get three shoe boxes, or cardboard the shape of a traffic light.
- Make three circles, one red, one orange and one yellow.
- Stick a circle on each of the boxes. Or stick all three on the cardboard traffic light shape.
- Attach a separate piece of paper over each of the circles, so that you can open the paper like a door. This is so that you can make the traffic light change colors.
- Get one long stick (this could be a broom/mop handle).
- Make a traffic light by putting the three shoe boxes together on the stick, or by attaching the cardboard traffic light to the stick.
- Get some artist tape and use it to make roads on the floor.

Things you can do with your traffic light

- Stand it up. Make it have a red light, a red and amber light and then a green light. Name the colors as you do it.
- Prop up the traffic light at the end of a road showing a red light. Ride a car down the road. Bring it to a stop. Then change the light to green and roll the car onwards.
- Have fun doing this with different cars.

Things you could invite your child/adult to do

- Roll a car down the streets and obey the traffic light (which you are controlling).
- Control the traffic light while you roll a car down the street.
- Pretend to be a car rolling down the street and stopping at the traffic light.
- Tell you what the color of the traffic light should be.
- Help you make different roads and junctions with the tape.
- Watch you change the traffic light.
- Make their own traffic light.
- Help stick the colors of the lights on.
- Color each circle.

MAKE A MAP GAME

Here are some suggestions of different maps you could create:

- Your house layout (i.e., floor plan). If your child/adult is into it you can measure each room. Hide treasure somewhere in the house. Mark an "X" where the treasure is.
- Grandma's house layout.
- Their school layout.
- A map of the room you are in—draw in all the objects that are in the room.
- A map of the moon:
  - Create different alien map symbols in "moon" language.

- Make a key at the right-hand side of the page. For example:
  - » Alien school is a star.
  - » Moon seas are marked by purple circles as all water on the moon is purple.
  - » Moon Library is marked by a yellow leaf.
  - » Moon Super Store is marked by the logo MSS.
- A map of a funfair with all the different rides.
- A map of the contents of your fridge.
- A map of their favorite highway.

Things you could invite your child/adult to do

- Watch you make the map.
- Tell you what to draw on the map.
- Draw the map themselves.
- Find where the treasure is.
- Make a map of your house and hide some treasure for you to find.

DECORATE ROAD SIGNS

- Print out a bunch of road signs.
- Cut them out.
- Get a bunch of stickers and decorate the signs with stickers.

MAKE UP NEW AND UNIQUE ROAD SIGNS FOR YOUR HOUSE

For example:

- A big arrow that says, "Kitchen this way."
- One for the kitchen door symbolizing, "Watch out! Hungry people could be near."
- One that says, "Beware! Monsters at play," outside their bedroom or playroom.

Things you could invite your child/adult to do

- Color in the signs.
- Stick them up on the walls around your house.
- Watch you make them.
- Come up with different ideas for different signs.

SHOWTIME IT

SILLY ROAD SIGN SHOW

- Download silly/crazy road signs from around the world and show them to your child/adult. For example, here are a few I found:
  - "Elephants please stay in your car."
  - "Beware of road surprises."
  - "Danger ahead! Fasten seatbelts and take out dentures."

Things you could invite your child/adult to do

- Sit beside you as you look at them.
- Read them to you.
- Listen as you read them.
- Make up their own silly road sign.
- Tell you their favorite.
- Point to the one they like the best.

SPONTANEOUS MAP TREASURE HUNT

- Hide a few things in the house or room that you are in with your child/adult. Hide something your child/adult likes—a stuffed animal, a Lego piece, a snack, a "map."
- Stick a big poster board on the wall.
- Explain that you have hidden "X" in the room—show a

picture of the item to your child/adult and tell them
about it.
- Start drawing a map of the room the treasure is in.
  It doesn't have to be fancy—a square for the shape
  of the room—another square where the table is, a
  square where the windows are and so on.
- Put the picture on the map where the item is.
- Either your child/adult will go and get it or you will.
- Then go on to the next item.

SUBWAY CITY ANNOUNCER GAME

- Make a line across the floor with artist tape. This
  symbolizes a subway line.
- Tape a few branches off to the left and right of the
  line. These branches are going to be subway stations.
- Decide what subway line you will use. For Londoners,
  it may be the "Piccadilly Line"; for New Yorkers it may
  be the "A train"; in the Amsterdam Metro, it may be
  the "M50" line.
- Write the names of the stations on this line on a piece
  of paper.
- You are the station announcer for the train.
- Wear a cap and hold a whistle.
- Either your child/adult walks down the line or gets
  into a cardboard box train that you push.
- As they approach each station you:
  - announce the station name
  - announce what other subway lines you can travel on
    from this station
  - hold up the station sign
  - tell them to mind the gap when leaving the train
  - once anyone has left the train and the doors are
    closed, announce what type of train it is and what the
    next station will be
  - make a train sound as it starts again
  - repeat the steps for all the stations.

Things you could invite your child/adult to do

- Help people (figurines/stuffed animals) on and off the train.
- Sit in the train while you push it along the line.
- Look at you while you announce the different train stations.
- Become the announcer.
- Make a new subway line.
- Roll toy subway trains along the line.

SUPERFACT IT

RESEARCH INTERESTING FACTS ABOUT MAPS, ROAD SIGNS, TRAFFIC LIGHTS AND SUBWAYS

Here are some topics to inspire you:

- Who invented the traffic light?
- Do all countries have the same traffic light system? Do traffic lights look different in each country?
- What did the first traffic light look like?
- What is shown on the oldest known map?
- Is there a map of space, and if so, what does it look like?
- What were the first-ever road signs?
- How are road signs different in different countries?
- Who gets to decide which road signs go up in your area?
- Will GPS make maps obsolete?
- The Highway Code in your country—download some driving test questions and answers.
- Which subway system was the first one to be built?
- What was the London Underground used for in World War II?

How you can use this information with your child/adult

Share it with your child/adult

- Have a discussion together about the information.
- Ask your child/adult what other information and facts they would be curious to know.
- As you talk, show them pictures related to your subject matter. Show the different maps and road signs.
- Share your thoughts and opinions on the information you found. Do you think it is interesting? Are there road signs in your town that you think should be put up? If so, what are they? If you could have one map to anywhere, where would it be?
- Talk about the rules of the road in your country, or have a quiz. Would you pass the driving test?

Name that Subway Line Gameshow

- Get ten pieces of paper.
- Write down a different subway line with all the station stops on that line on each piece of paper.
- Fold them up and put them in a bowl.
- You each take turns picking a piece of paper and asking the other person what the stations are on that line.
- If the guesser gets stuck, the reader can give them clues.
- How many will you get?
- Variation: Do the same game, but instead of a subway line, write a destination that your child/adult knows. With the starting point being your home, the guesser has to say how you would get there, by car, walking, subway or train.

Road sign Frisbee

- Print out road signs from many different countries.
- Stand on opposite sides of the room (or as far apart from each other as you can get).
- On each side of the room, put some printed-out road signs and a roll of tape.

- Start the game by taping a road sign onto the Frisbee and throwing it to your child/adult. (If you don't have a Frisbee, just use a ball that tape will stick to.)
- They try to catch it. Once it is caught, they get to see the road sign and tell you what it means. Then they tape a new road sign on the Frisbee and throw it back to you to say what it means.
- Keep going until all road signs are used up.
- Variation: Instead of using printed-out road signs, you each have blank paper and draw your own made-up road signs for the other person to guess.

Animals and Insects

BE IT

VERSION 1

- Act out being a dog (or your child/adult's favorite animal/insect). Really get into it. Get on all fours and run about. Stick out your tongue and pant, howl or bark like a dog.

VERSION 2

- Use face paints and paint your face as your child/adult's favorite animal/insect. If you become a lion, paint the whole of your face lion yellow with lion whiskers. You can look up animal faces online for inspiration (or for speedy preparation you can just use a mask).

VERSION 3

- Print out pictures of different animals: jungle insects, exotic big cats, polar bears.
- Tape them all over your body—on your chest, arms, legs and back.

Abracadabra! Three different ways to become an animal or insect.

Things you can do once you have become an animal or insect

For Versions 1 and 2

- Pretend to eat like the animal or insect would eat.
- If you are a dog, play fetch the ball, or roll over and play dead.
- Sing tunes in the sounds of the animal you are.
- Fly everywhere if you are an insect.

For Version 3

- Point to each animal picture and say their names.
- Point to one picture and make that animal's sound.
- Unstick one picture and chase your child/adult with it.
- Unstick one picture and stick it on your child/adult.
- Point to one picture and say a fun fact about that animal.

Things you could invite your child/adult to do

- Feed you.
- Pet you.
- Play fetch with you—throw a ball or stick for you to pick up.
- Become an animal with you.
- Have their face painted like yours, or wear the mask.
- Make their own antenna, tail or wings.
- Say the names of the animals.
- Cover themselves with pictures of animals.

MAKE IT/DRAW IT

HORSE BARN GAME

- Make a big barn for the horse.
- The barn is just two old sheets draped across furniture to create a den or fort.
- Put some yellow tissue/crepe paper on the floor as fake straw.

- Put some real or fake carrots and apples at the barn entrance in a bucket.
- Make some horse jumps out of bricks around the room.
- Get on all fours.
- Put a blanket on your back as a saddle.
- Neigh and trot around so that it is clear that you are a horse.
- Trot into the barn.
- Stick your head out and pretend to eat the carrots and apples just like a horse would.
- Come out again and do the horse jumps.

Things you could invite your child/adult to do

- Get on your back and go for a horse ride.
- Lead you by a rein around the horse-jumping course.
- Feed you the carrots or apples.
- Put out new straw for your barn floor.
- Be a horse with you.
- Come inside the barn with you.
- Brush you.
- Put new shoes on your hooves.

ANIMAL PICTURE CHASE GAME

- Print out free "coloring pages" from the internet of animals you will most likely want to run away from, such as a:
  - lion
  - tiger
  - scorpion
  - giant spider
  - big brown bear.
- Present the picture to your child/adult and start coloring it in.
- Then have the picture chase them.

- When you catch them, have the animal pretend to "eat" them.
- Repeat with a different animal.

Things you could invite your child/adult to do

- Color in the picture.
- Chase you with the picture.
- Pick the next animal to chase them.
- Watch you color in the picture.
- Point to the next color to use for coloring in.
- Give you the next coloring marker.

MAKE A MISMATCH ANIMAL GAME

- Get pictures of real animals.
- Cut them out and then cut them in half.
- Then mismatch one half of an animal with a different one, for example the head of a giraffe and a body of a dog; or the head of an elephant and the body of a bear.

Things you could invite your child/adult to do

- Give you different animal parts for the next mismatch animal.
- Make one of their own.
- Tape or glue them together.
- Tell you which animal to make.
- Give you a part of each animal for the next mismatch.
- Have a conversation about what that animal would be called.
- Watch you make the mismatch animals.

FIND THE FISH GAME

- Scrunch up 20 or more whole pieces of blue crepe paper or tissue paper, so that they fill a large space. They are the water in a pond.
- Print out pictures of ten tropical fish. And maybe a mermaid or two?
- Hide the fish among the scrunched-up pieces of paper.
- The game is to find the fish.
- Variations could be to use brown crepe/tissue paper and hide moles in the "earth." Or hide bunny rabbits who are down in their rabbit holes. Or worms.

Things you could invite your child/adult to do

- Find the fish.
- Count the fish.
- Say the names of the fish as they find them.
- Help you scrunch the paper for the pond.
- Hide the fish for you to find.
- Dive in and go swimming with the fish.
- Watch you find the fish.

SHOWTIME IT

TOUR GUIDE AT THE ZOO GAME

- Cut out photos of different zoo animals. Have at least three of each animal:
  - Giraffes
  - Lions
  - Parrots
  - Monkeys
  - Seals
  - Spiders.
- Stick the pictures up on different walls in your room. Or put each collection of animals up on the wall in

different rooms in your house. The whole house is the zoo.

- Have a toy megaphone, or microphone, or use a wooden spoon as a pretend microphone.
- Get an umbrella and put it up when you move from animal section to animal section, so that "everyone" can see you as you guide them around the zoo.
- Walk over to the collection of animals and present what they are to your child/adult. You could say something like:
  - "And here we have Malik, Daisy and Tanny, the giraffes." Make up their ages and hobbies. For example, "Malik likes to nibble on your ears, and Daisy likes to spit out water, while Tanny likes to read." Then act out those hobbies.
  - If necessary, lift your child up to see the pictures of the animals.
- Move on to the next set of animals and present these in the same way.

Other things you could do at the zoo

- Create a gift shop that sells pictures of the animals, or plastic figurines.
- Ride your child on your back from animal section to animal section.
- Pull them on a wagon.
- Have them bounce to each new animal section on a big therapy ball.
- Have pictures of animal food your child/adult can give to the animals; for example, fish for the seals.
- When you get to the animal section and show the picture, pretend to be that animal.

Things you could invite your child/adult to do

- Look at the animals.
- Point to the animals.

- Say hello to the animals.
- Wave hello to the animals.
- Get on your back to ride to the next animal section.
- Feed the animals.
- Make the animal sounds.
- Pretend to be the animals.
- Name the animals.
- Talk to the animals.
- Answer the animals' questions.
- Buy something in the gift shop.
- Draw a picture of the animals.

FLYING PIGS AND JUMPING FROGS GAME

- Get some frog figures or soft animals, or just some pictures of frogs.
- For the pictures, draw wings on them.
- For the figurines and soft animals, make tissue paper wings and tape them onto the figures or stuffed animals.
- Get as many as possible.
- Do the same for the pigs.
- Get a couple of buckets and put them around the room.
- Announce that it is flying pig and frog season.
- Then make them fly into the buckets:
  - Throw them high into the air (aiming at the buckets).
  - Launch them into the air with a bat or racket (aiming at the buckets).
  - Launch them with a sling shot (aiming at the buckets).

Things you could invite your child/adult to do

- Give you the frogs or pigs to fly.
- Tell you which animal to fly.
- Watch you fly them into the bucket.
- Count how many you got into the buckets and how many you missed.
- Keep score for you and for them.

- Pick up the ones you missed and hand them to you so that you can try again.
- Make more wings for the frogs and pigs.
- Try flying them into the buckets themselves.

ANIMAL MUSICAL THEATRE GAME

- Pick a song from the links below.
- Stick pictures of the animals you are singing about on your shirt. Or dress up as one of the animals.
- Do the actions with enthusiasm and animation as you sing them.
- Below are links to songs that are super easy to learn and have actions:
  - https://youtu.be/CT86Dl442jA
  - https://youtu.be/3OePPeUbwSs
  - https://youtu.be/HpOe8lngp_o
  - https://youtu.be/BfUoopDpmmY
  - https://youtu.be/IkanoEmIcHM
  - https://youtu.be/pWepfJ-8XUO
  - https://youtu.be/Imhi98dHa5w

Note: These are for you to watch and learn the songs to sing to your child/adult.

SUPERFACT IT

RESEARCH INTERESTING FACTS ABOUT ANIMALS AND INSECTS

Here are some topics to inspire you:

- How many species are there in the animal kingdom?
- How many different species of insects are there?
- Name all the different kinds of frogs there are by country. (There are endless animals to do this with. Just pick one at a time.)

- How many different kinds of sharks are there?
- What animals are in danger of being extinct soon?
- What animals were around in the 1900s that are now extinct?
- What is the largest animal?
- What is the smallest animal?
- How many zoos are there in your country? And what animals do they have?
- Who has the largest collection of pets in the world and what are they?

How you can use this information with your child/adult

Share it with your child/adult

- Have a discussion together about the information.
- Ask your child/adult what other information and facts they would be curious to know about animals.
- Show them pictures of what you are talking about.
- Share your thoughts and opinions on the information you found. Do you think it is interesting? Do you like some animals? Are you scared of others? Which animals would you like to meet? If you were an animal, what animal would you be?

Name as Many Kinds as You Can game

- Get a timer—a cooking timer would work well.
- Write out these challenges:
  1. Name as many different kinds of dogs as you can.
  2. Name as many different kinds of cats as you can.
  3. Name as many different kinds of fish as you can.
  4. Name as many different kinds of crawling insects as you can.
  5. Name as many different kinds of birds as you can.
  6. Name as many different kinds of flying insects as you can.
  7. Name as many animals that lay eggs as you can.
  8. Name as many different kinds of animals that make their nest in a tree as you can.
  9. Name as many different kinds of horses as you can.

10. Name as many different kinds of monkeys as you can.

- Add to this list, as you want to.
- Each person gets one minute to name as many as they can. The listener writes them down or counts them until the timer goes off.

Create a poster to raise awareness about endangered species

- For example, this could be about bees.
- You could both do your own poster or collaborate on one together.
- If it is a collaboration, the following things need to be agreed on:
  - What will the artwork for the poster be? It could be:
    » hand drawn
    » cut-out pictures
    » photos you take yourself, such as real bees in your garden or park
    » painted.
  - What is it going to say?
  - What action do you want people to do to save the bees?
- Once it is made, you can make phone calls together to ask family members or friends if they are willing to put the poster up in their house, store or workplace.

What Animal Am I?

- This is a simple fun charades game.
- Put pictures of different animals in a bowl. Each picture has a fun fact about that animal on the back.
- You each take turns picking one out.
- You each get three minutes to act it out, being that animal doing the fun fact on the back of the card.
- If it has not been guessed by the end of the three minutes, the guesser gets to ask three "yes/no" questions to help them guess.

Cell Phones

BE IT

VERSION 1

- Print a screenshot of your phone's home screen.
- Attach it to your shirt. You are a human phone.

VERSION 2

- Get a piece of paper and tape a "video" icon on it.
- Write the words "VIDEO CALL" in capital letters at the top of the piece of paper. Underneath these words, draw a big box.
- Get different pictures of family members or cartoon/movie characters your child/adult likes, or different animals (i.e., use your child/adult's motivations) and put this on your shirt. You are going to become a human video chat room.
- Make the sound of your video chat system (e.g., Facetime/Signal/WhatsApp).
- Put a picture in the box and have a pretend conversation.
- Switch to another picture and chat again.

VERSION 3

- Print out either one big YouTube icon or lots of little ones.
- Stick them all over yourself.
- Press the YouTube icon and start acting out your child/adult's favorite YouTube show. You are the show.

Abracadabra! Three different ways to become a cell phone.

Things you can do once you have become a cell phone/app

For Version 1

- Press an app and make the sound it makes. For example:
  - A call tone for the phone app
  - Saying the directions for the map app in the app voice
  - The "click" of a text for the text app
  - Sounds for any other app you know your child/adult likes.

For Version 2

- Have a fun conversation with your video app partner:
  - Interview an animal, or family member or movie character.
  - Have an animal sound conversation. For example, the conversation could be entirely in pig snorts or duck quacks.
  - Call someone up on the video app and tell them some jokes.
  - Call someone up and show them some pictures.
  - Call someone up and read them a story.

For Version 3

- Act out your child/adult's favorite show.
- Make your own version of a YouTube channel. It could be called "Mom's corner" or "Dad's wisdom," where you share a wise tip or cool fact.
- Act out being in a music video.

- Pretend you are joining a YouTube yoga class, or a dance or keep-fit class.
- The possibilities are limitless!

Things you could invite your child/adult to do

- Press an app icon.
- Tell you which icon to press/be.
- Act out a song/show with you.
- Tell you who to call next on your video phone.
- Be the person you call.
- Become the phone themselves.
- Choose the app icon to stick on themselves.
- Be an audience for your great entertainment.
- Watch you acting things out or doing the video call.

MAKE IT/DRAW IT

DESIGN YOUR OWN PHONE APP

You come up with an idea first. Here is a list of possibilities to inspire you:

- An app that creates pictures of your favorite toys doing funny things.
- An app that sounds an alarm every time the fridge opens, and a family member eats the last cookie or bowl of cereal or sip of milk.
- An app that takes a picture of your face and superimposes it onto famous movie scenes, so you become the star of the show.

Things you can do once you pick the app idea

- Design the logo for the app.
- Mock up a few logo designs and get all your family members to pick their favorite.

- Make a list of everything you need to do to make an app.
- Choose the theme music for the app.
- Make the layout of all the pages in the app.
- What would the content be on each of the pages?

MAKE A HOME SCREEN POSTER

- Get a big poster board.
- Print out lots of different phone/app icons.
- Put the icons in different envelopes, one in each envelope.
- Open an envelope and show your child/adult what is inside.
- Stick it on the poster.
- Open another and then stick it on, and so on.

Things you can do once the Home Screen Poster is made

- Act out that particular app. For example, "click" on the phone icon and pretend you are calling Mom or Dad, or that you are calling your child/adult's favorite character.
- Point to each app and name it.
- Point to each app and make the "sounds" of that app. For example:
    - The ring tone of your phone
    - The ring tone of Facetime
    - The click of your text
    - A song from your music app.

Things you could invite your child/adult to do

- Give you an envelope.
- Open the envelope.
- Stick the envelope on the poster.
- Say the name of the icon they find in the envelope.

MAKE CELL PHONES

- Get some thick card (old cardboard boxes work well).
- Draw around your phone so you make the phones the same size as your phone.
- Cut out two of the phones, one for each of you.
- If your child/adult has a favorite soft toy or object or imaginary friend, make one for that person/toy too.
- Print out a version of the home screen of your phone.
- If you have old phone cases, bring those too.
- You now have completed pieces of a cell phone ready to assemble.
- Model each step in putting a phone together first.
- Then assemble another.

Things you could invite your child/adult to do

- Watch you put the phones together.
- Give you the different parts to assemble.
- Stick the home screens to the cardboard.
- Put the cardboard phones into the old cases.

Things you can do once the cell phones are made

- Give one each to your child/adult and the toys or soft animals.
- Call up the animals or toys that have a phone and have a conversation with them. You talk through your phone and then you act out the soft animal or toy talking back.
- For the rest of your interaction time, say everything while talking on the phone (you and them).

SHOWTIME IT

APP STORE GAME

- Create a poster covered with app icons you made up. To make it easy, the app icons can be just the first letter of what the app is about. For example, a joke app would be just a large "J," a nonsense rhyming app would be just "NR" and so on. Think up apps that your child/adult might like that you could perform for them.

- To give you some ideas, here are a few suggestions:
  - Mickey Mouse app
  - Joke app
  - Sound effects app
  - Ride app
  - Song app
  - Tickle app
  - Weatherman app
  - Thunder app
  - Math app
  - Nonsense rhyming app
  - Story-telling app.
- Each time you or your child/adult points to an app icon you tell them the name of the app, and:
  - tell a bunch of jokes, if it is the joke app
  - sing, if it is the song app
  - give your child or a soft animal a ride, if it is the ride app
  - pretend to be Mickey Mouse or draw Mickey Mouse, if it is the Mickey Mouse app.

Things you could invite your child/adult to do

- Watch you act out the apps.
- Point to an app they want you to act out.
- Make a new app to add to the poster.
- Act out one of the apps; for example, tell a joke or sing a song.
- Get a ride themselves in the ride app.
- Verbally tell you which app to do next.

YOUTUBE APP GAME

- Print out the YouTube icon.
- Print out thumbnails of YouTube videos that your child/adult likes to watch. (Make sure you watch them before, so you know what is in each one.)
- Put them in your pockets.
- Take them out one at a time and stick each one on your chest.
- Act out what is happening in the video.
- Sing what is being sung in the video.
- Have the soft animals help you act them out.
- Have the toy vehicles act out what is happening in the video.

Things you could invite your child/adult to do

- Just be the audience and watch you act it out.
- Tell you what you missed in acting it out.
- Tell you what to act out next.
- Act out the video with you.
- Be the audio of the video.
- Point to the video they want you to do next.
- Clap at the end of the video show.

WRITE CELL PHONE SONGS

Make up some songs about cell phones. Here are some titles to help inspire you:

- "Ten Reasons Why I Love My Phone." Here are the first five reasons for inspiration:
    - Because I like my ring tone. It goes... (sing the sound)
    - Because I can watch YouTube on my phone
    - Because it does what I want it to do
    - Because it has my favorite game on it
    - Because I get to watch [X] on it.

- "Ten Reasons Why My Parents Hate My Phone"
- "Android Versus iPhone."

Things you and your child/adult could do

- Write the whole song yourself and sing it to your child/adult.
- Write the first three lines and sing those to them and have them come up with the rest.
- Create actions to go along with the song.
- Create the first three actions and then ask your child/adult to come up with the actions for the rest of the song.
- Do your song to the beat and tune of a popular song.
- Do it as a rap.
- Tap dance when you sing it.
- Do hip hop when you sing it.
- For "Ten Reasons..." songs, you could stick pieces of paper all over you with numbers on them. Pull number 1 off and give it to your child/adult as you sing reason number 1, then pull number 2 off and give it to your child/adult as you sing reason number 2, and so on.

SUPERFACT IT

RESEARCH INTERESTING FACTS ABOUT CELL PHONES

Here are some topics for inspiration:

- How many different brands of cell phone are there?
- How many models/upgrades have there been for each brand?
- What are the differences between the upgrades?
- Which brand has the latest technology?
- What is something an iPhone has that an Android does not?
- What is something an Android has that an iPhone does not?

- Which brand sells the most smartphones?
- Where do they rank in terms of cost?
- Who came out with the very first cell phone?
- Who came out with the very first smartphone?
- How big was the very first cell phone?
- How did cell phones evolve to where we are today with the small handheld smartphone?
- How is a smartphone made?
- Find out as many facts as you can about the original developer of the iPhone or the Android.
- Where are the cell phone factories?
- How big are the cell phone factories?
- What happens to all the old cell phones?

How you can use this information with your child/adult

Share one topic from these amazing facts with them

- Read out each fact.
- Pretend you are a presenter on a TV show, sharing the facts about cell phones.
- After sharing the facts, you could have a discussion about them.

Make a future upgrade advertisement

- Share all the latest facts about the latest iPhone and then make up what the next upgrade will be.
- Include ideas from your child/adult.
- Make an advertisement together for the future upgrade.

Guess Which Model This Is Card Game

- Print out different pictures of cell phones:
  - Old ones
  - Current ones
  - Different brands.
- Stick them on some card with the make and model on the back.

- Put them face up on the table.
- The game is for you each to have a go at guessing the make and model of each one.
- How many do you each guess?

Phone Memory Game

- Get a regular pack of cards.
- Take 20 of the cards.
- Take ten pictures of different iPhone models and print out two pictures of each model.
- Stick one to each of the cards.
- Turn them face down on the table and each take turns turning over two to find a match.
- How many matches do you each get?

Cell Phone Trivia Night

- You can do this with just your child/adult on the spectrum or with other family members as well.
- Each of you creates your own trivia questions from the information you have already researched. about cell phones. For example, "What make and model of cell phone is the most expensive?" or "How many different versions of cell phone have Apple come out with to date?" You could even add a personal one such as "What cell phone does your grandma have?"
- You each make up six questions.
- Once you have each created the questions, before you ask them, decide ahead of time how many the other person will get right and how many they might not know. Write down your guesses and put them in a sealed envelope.
- Then you each take turns asking each other the trivia questions, keeping score of how many were answered correctly and incorrectly.
- At the end, open the envelopes to reveal how close your guesses were.

Movies, Cartoons and TV Shows

BE IT

VERSION 1

- Dress up as a character from your child/adult's favorite movie, cartoon or TV show.
- Make the best costume you can, and have some props too.

VERSION 2

- Print out the faces of different characters from your child/adult's favorite movie, cartoon or TV show, or cut them out from magazines.
- Stick them all over your body.

VERSION 3

- Get an old TV remote control.
- Print out the names of all your child/adult's favorite TV programs, movies and cartoons.
- Write them on a poster board.
- Punch two holes at the top of the poster board.

- Attach a string through the holes so you can hang the poster around your neck.
- Press the remote control and point to one of the movie titles. Say the title out loud and then quote lines from the movie.

Abracadabra! Three different ways to become a movie, cartoon or TV show.

Things you can do once you have become a movie, cartoon or TV show

For Version 1

- Talk and walk like that character.
- Dance like that character.
- Sing the theme tune or a song from the movie, cartoon or TV show.
- Introduce yourself as the character, in the voice of the character, to your child/adult.
- Act out a scene from the movie, cartoon or TV show.
- Pretend one of the puppets is interviewing you and answer their questions. For inspiration, here are some of the questions the puppet could ask you:
  - What do you like about being famous?
  - What is your favorite line in the movie?
  - Can I have your autograph?
  - What is your favorite song from the movie?
  - Can I have your tiara [or any other part of your dressing-up costume]?
  - What do you eat for breakfast?
  - Where do you live, and can I come over?
  - How could I become an extra on a movie?

For Version 2

- Pull off two or three of the characters and act out a scene from the movie, cartoon or TV show between those characters.

- Pull off one character and then say in the character's voice, "Where are you [add the name of another character]?" and then find that character on your body, pull it off and have that character say another character's name until all of them have been pulled off.

For Version 3

- Keep pressing the remote control and saying quotes from the different movies, cartoons and TV shows that are written on your poster board.
- After pressing the remote and pointing to the title:
  - Say the name of the movie, cartoon of TV show.
  - Sing the theme song.
  - Do a dance routine from the movie, cartoon or TV show.
  - Talk in the voice of one of the characters.

Things you could invite your child/adult to do

For Version 1

- Sing a song with you.
- Act out a scene with you.
- Interview you in character.
- Watch you act out scenes.
- Watch you sing.
- Try on your costume.
- Tell you what to sing, say or act out.

For Version 2

- Name all the characters that are stuck on you.
- Look at all the characters stuck on you.
- Pull all of them off.
- Stick them on themselves.
- Say lines that the characters would say.

For Version 3

- Press the remote control.
- Say the names of all the movies, cartoons or TV show.
- Sing with you.
- Dance with you.
- Say a line from the movie, cartoon or TV show.
- Watch you as you sing, dance or recite lines from the movie, cartoon or TV show.

MAKE IT/DRAW IT

MOVIE PROP GAME

- Make a special "prop" from your child/adult's favorite movie. It could be:
  - a light sabre from *Star Wars*
  - the ring from *The Lord of the Rings*
  - the apple in *Snow White*
  - a car from the *Cars* movie
  - the magical mirror from *Beauty and the Beast*
  - a wand or Quidditch stick from the *Harry Potter* movies
  - a guitar from the *Troll* movies.
- Use the prop to recreate a scene from the movie that centers around it.
- Create a game with that prop at the center. Here is an example:

BEAUTY AND THE BEAST MIRROR PROP GAME
This game was made up by a fabulously creative mom called Joni who used the Magical Mirror as the prop.

- She used a handheld plastic mirror.
- She looked into the mirror and said to the mirror, "I want to see Beauty." She then twirled herself around and with her

back to her daughter stuck a picture of Beauty on the mirror and turned back around, looked at the mirror and showed it to her daughter.

- She continued to ask the mirror to show her other characters from the movie. She said, "I want to see the Candlestick." She twirled around, with her back to her daughter, and stuck a picture of the Candlestick onto the mirror, twirled back and looked in the mirror and showed her daughter.
- Then she turned to her daughter and asked her what character from *Beauty and the Beast* does she want to see? Tell the mirror and they will appear.

Things you could invite your child/adult to do

- Watch you as you demonstrate the game.
- Say a character they want to see.
- Take the picture of the mirror.
- Add a picture to the mirror.

CARTOON REMAKE GAME

- Print out your child/adult's favorite cartoon.
- Cut all the cartoon squares up so that they are separate.
- Number each section on the back so you know which order the story goes in.
- Stick the first cartoon square on the wall.
- Put the rest of the cartoon squares on a shelf or in your pocket.
- Read what the cartoon characters are saying to each other in the first square.
- Get the next cartoon square and stick that one up.
- Read that cartoon square.
- Keep doing the same until the whole cartoon story is taped up on the wall in a long line.

- If your child/adult likes this, do it again with a different cartoon story.
- Variation: Draw each scene out on a handheld whiteboard or chalk board.

Things you could invite your child/adult to do

- Look at the story as you stick each cartoon square up.
- Listen to you reading what the characters are saying to each other.
- Read the cartoon squares themselves.
- Tell you which square should come next.
- Help you stick the next square onto the wall.

FINISH THE PICTURE GAME

- Print out two copies of a scene from your child/adult's favorite movie, cartoon or TV show. Or cut one out of a magazine and photocopy it.
- Take one of the printouts and cut out part of the picture. Maybe you cut off half a character (e.g., their head and shoulders or their legs), or one of the characters entirely. Maybe you cut off a tree or a car that is in the scene—just a little part of the scene.
- Stick the scene that you have cut part out of onto a poster board or sheet of paper.
- Show your child/adult both pictures, the full scene and the scene with a part cut out.
- The game is to draw back the missing piece.
- Do it again with another scene.

Things you could invite your child/adult to do

- Point to the part of the picture that is missing.
- Watch you draw the missing piece back in.
- Draw the missing piece back in themselves.
- Tell you what is missing.

SHOWTIME IT

TV SHOW PUPPETS

- Print out or photocopy the faces of different characters from your child/adult's favorite TV show. This could mean making quite a lot of characters if their favorite is say, *Paw Patrol*, for example. But your child/adult just may know them all!
- Stick the faces on the top of popsicle sticks.
- You now have a bunch of popsicle puppets!
- Create a puppet show of a scene from one of their favorite episodes.
- Use just a few or all of the characters.
- Create a puppet show of some characters singing a song.
- Create a puppet show of the characters doing regular things like brushing their teeth or going to bed.

Things you could invite your child/adult to do

- Name the characters.
- Point to the character you name.
- Hold the popsicle puppets.
- Be the voice of one of the puppets.
- Watch you put on a show.
- Hand you a certain character when it is their turn to star in the show.
- Make scenery for the puppet show.
- Star in the puppet show themselves.
- Put on the puppet show themselves.
- Be the director of the puppet show.
- Make the popsicle puppets with you.

MOVIE MUSICAL HOLIDAY SPECIAL

- There is always a holiday somewhere in the world that you can celebrate. There are so many to choose from—Easter, Fourth of July, Hanukkah, Christmas, Eid al-Fitr, Holi, Kwanzaa, Qingming Festival, Chinese New Year and more.
- You can celebrate a holiday in your culture or discover one from another culture.
- Put on a Musical Holiday Special.
- Decorate the room in the decorations from the particular holiday you are celebrating. It does not matter if it is close to that day or not. If you are doing a Christmas special, put up Christmas lights. If it is Chinese New Year, put up paper lanterns and paper dragons.
- Use a medley of songs from your child/adult's favorite musical movies.
- If they have dance routines in the movies, learn parts of them and dance as well.
- Get a pretend microphone, or karaoke machine if you have one.
- Sing and dance your heart out.

Things you could invite your child/adult to do

- Watch you put up the decorations.
- Help you put up the decorations.
- Hum along.
- Listen to you sing.
- Sing parts of or all of the songs with you.
- Tell you which song to sing next.
- Watch you dance.
- Do some of the dance steps or actions with you.
- Learn all of the dance moves.

SUPERFACT IT

RESEARCH INTERESTING FACTS ABOUT MOVIES, CARTOONS AND TV SHOWS

Specifically find out about the particular one(s) that your child/adult likes. Here are some topics to inspire your research:

- What was the first movie ever made?
- Did Disney create the first animated movie? If not, who did?
- What was the first animated movie?
- How do cartoons get made?
- What TV show is the longest running in history?
- How have TV game shows developed over time?
- How many movies have been made about the same story (e.g., Cinderella)?
- What movie has the most sequels?
- What movie has the largest number of extras?
- How are movie special effects created?
- How do moviemakers create and maneuver, for example, the big dinosaurs in *Jurassic Park*? Or the robots in *Star Wars*?
- Research about the history of stunt men and find pictures of your child/adult's favorite actor and their double.
- What have been some of the most famous or influential movie or TV documentaries?

How to use this information with your child/adult

Share it with your child/adult

- Have a discussion together about all the information you find.
- Ask them what other information and facts they would be curious to know about any movies, cartoons or TV shows.
- Show them pictures you have found of what you are talking about.

- Share your thoughts and opinions on the information you found. Do you think it is interesting? Do you like silent movies? Are movies better in black and white? How would you feel if big movie theaters disappeared? Do you prefer the movie theater or a drive-in theater? Do you prefer live action movies or animated movies?

Design your own TV game show

- Design your own brand-new TV game show together.
- Discuss and answer the following questions to help you create it:
  - What will the game be:
    » A word game?
    » A bowling game?
    » A math game?
    » A bird/song/mountain game?
  - Write out the questions and the rules.
  - Who will be the host?
  - Who will be the participants?
  - How many people will play at once?
  - What will they win?
- Invite family members to play, or use the figurines and stuffed animals as participants.
- Have fun playing it.

Film your own documentary

- Use a regular camcorder (one that is not connected to the internet).
- Decide whether it will be silent or with sound.
- Choose the documentary style:
  - Interview style, where the documentary is based on several interviews with the subject of the documentary
  - A day in the life of the subject, where you follow your subject around and film them going about their daily life.
- Choose your subject. Will it be a family member, an animal or your garden?
- If you choose an interview style, come up with the questions

and approach the subject for consent and interview times. Then film it. One of you is the camera operator; the other is the interviewer.

- If it is a day in the life of your subject, ask for permission to film them at certain times during the day. Then film them or it at those times.
- If you do not find someone who will agree to be your subject, be each other's subject.

Things that Dangle, Drop or Spin

There are so many things your child/adult might like to watch dangle, drop or spin. It might be belts, string, hair, ribbons, hands, plates, wheels, fans.

BE IT

DANGLING THING: VERSION 1

- Cut up a bunch of ribbon all similar length. Split this into two bunches.
- Tie a knot at one end of each bunch.
- Attach each one to a hairband or rubber band.
- Put them on your wrists.

DANGLING THING: VERSION 2

- Get a bunch of belts and tie them around one or both of your arms.
- Tie them so that a long piece will dangle down when you put your arms straight out in front of you. (You could also use string, or a long piece of wool.)

DANGLING THING: VERSION 3

- If you have any clothes that already have the Country and Western style fringe on them, wear them.
- If you don't, make your own long paper fringe clothes by:
  - taking a piece of paper and cutting lots of lines down one side that do not reach the other side
  - taping these to your shirt sleeves, trouser legs and the bottom of your shirt. You have your very own cowboy/girl fringe clothes!

Abracadabra! Three different ways to become a human dangling thing.

Things you can do once you have become an object that dangles

For Version 1

- Move your arms around in circles, in front of you and above your head.
- Put your hands together to make one big bunch of ribbons and shake them standing in one spot, and as you move your hands in a figure-of-eight.
- Put your hands up on top of your head so that the ribbons lie on your head like hair. Shake your head back and forth.
- Chase your child/adult while shaking the ribbons.
- Chase and catch your child/adult. Once you have caught them, tickle them with the ribbons.

For Version 2

- Put your arms straight out to the side and move your arms so that the belts gently swing in the air.
- Spin the belts as fast as you can in a full circle.
- Run around the room with your arms out as if you are flying, and allow the belts to move as they wish.

For Version 3

- Move your arms in the air.
- Sway them back and forth.
- Jump up and down.
- Do the chicken dance so that your fringe or paper fringe moves.

Things you could invite your child/adult to do

- Watch the ribbons/belts and fringes move.
- Dance with you.
- Say, "dance," "shake" or "move."
- Make their own paper fringe clothes.
- Point to the fringe or belt or ribbon they want you to shake or move.
- Run through the ribbons so they touch their face.
- Run away from you so that you can chase them.
- Say, "tickle" or "chase."

SPINNING THING: VERSION 1

- Get a big hula hoop and spin it on your arm. If you have two, put one on each arm and spin both at the same time.
- If you do not have hula hoops you can use the hoops from a ring toss game. Put all of them on your arms and spin them.

SPINNING THING: VERSION 2

- Get several plastic plates.
- Take five or more and start spinning them on the floor.
- Keep them spinning for a long as you can.
- You are the mad spinning plate professor.

SPINNING THING: VERSION 3

- Get some paper/plastic pinwheels.
- If you want to make your own, here is a link that will show you how you can do that: https://youtu.be/CORugzrpgv8
- Pin the pinwheels all over your shirt and trousers.
- You are a giant spinning festival of delight.

Abracadabra! Three different ways to become a spinning thing.

Things you can do once you have become a spinning thing

- Spin the hula hoops, plates or pinwheels as much as you can. See if you can get a good rhythm going and become a spinning spectacle.
- Show a lot of delight as you spin. Laugh, sing, smile and really enjoy it.
- Spin or walk in circles as you spin the plates/hula hoops/pinwheels.

Things you could invite your child/adult to do

- Look at you to indicate they want you to spin the plates/pin-wheels/hula hoops some more.
- Spin/blow the pinwheels on your shirt or trousers.
- Spin the hula hoops.
- Tell you to spin the plate.
- Point to the plate or hula hoop or pinwheel for you to spin.
- Tell you how many plates to spin at one time.
- Put the pinwheels on themselves.

MAKE IT/DRAW IT

MAKE POMPOMS

- Get a few sheets of tissue/crepe paper—around ten sheets.
- Cut all the sheets into a long strip about 12 inches long and 1 inch wide.
- Put all the 12-inch strips together.
- Put masking tape around the middle of the strips so that it keeps them together.
- Hold the masking tape part in your hand and shake it.
- It's a pompom!
- Make four—two for you and two for your child/adult.

Things to do with the pompoms

- Throw them high in the air. See if they can touch the ceiling.
- Chase your child and tickle them with the pompom.
- Do a pompom dance. Here's one idea for inspiration:
  - Holding both pompoms, shake them to the left.
  - Shake them to the right.
  - Shake them to the left.
  - Shake them to the right.
  - Shake them over your head.
  - Jump three times.
  - Holding your pompoms, bend your elbows so that they are both pointed outwards. To the count of three, move the pompoms in a circular motion around one another.
  - Repeat.
- Put some sticker eyes on them and make them into monster pompom heads.

Things you could invite your child/adult to do

- Watch you do the pompom dance.
- Watch you throw the pompoms in the air.
- Do a pompom dance step.

- Say, "pompom."
- Pick up the pompom and give it back to you to throw in the air.
- Make their own pompom.
- Be chased by the pompom monster.
- Name the pompom monster.

GIANT SPINNER POSTER GAME OF DELIGHT

- Draw a big circle as big as you can on a poster board.
- Divide it into six sections, each section being the shape of a slice of cake.
- In each section, write the name or stick a picture of an object that you can spin for your child/adult. Here are some suggestions:
  - Red plastic bowl
  - Yellow plastic plate
  - Spinning top
  - A pinwheel
  - Yourself
  - Your child.
- Tape the very top of the pinwheel stick to the poster board so that the pinwheel head is right at the center of the circle. Make sure you tape the top of the stick of the pinwheel so that the pinwheel can spin.
- Move the pinwheel with your hands to make sure it can spin.
- Take one of the corners of the pinwheel's petals and stick something on it so it looks different from the other ones. This could be a sticker, or you could draw a colored shape on it.
- When you spin the pinwheel, the petal that has the sticker on it will land in a particular section. If it lands in the section with the words or picture of the yellow plate, you get the yellow plate and spin it for your child/adult. If it lands on the spinning top, you spin that. If it lands on you, you spin. If it lands on them, you spin them.

Things you could invite your child/adult to do

- Spin the spinner.
- Watch you spin the spinner.
- Watch you spin what it lands on.
- Add a new object to spin to the game board.
- Take turns with you spinning the board and spinning things.
- Say, "spin the spinner."
- Tell you what to spin.
- Make another spinning poster board with different objects on it.

BUCKET DROP GAME

- Get two buckets.
- Fill one with six ping-pong balls.
- Fill the other with tiny scrunched up pieces of tissue. (Or fill them with the specific things your child/adult likes to watch drop or fall.)
- Stand on the sofa or table or at the top of a step ladder, somewhere where you can drop the things from the bucket at a good height. Your child/adult will get to see the things fall for longer.
- Pour out the ping-pong balls from that height.
- Pour out the tiny scrunched up pieces of tissue.
- Gather them up and repeat.

Things you could invite your child/adult to do

- Watch you pour the contents of the bucket from a height.
- Say, "pour," "ping pongs," "tissues," "drop," "fall."
- Give you the buckets to do it again.
- Put the objects back in the bucket so you can pour again.
- Watch you climb the step ladder.
- Tell you other things you could drop from that height.

SHOWTIME IT

WISH UPON A STAR GAME

- Cut out star shapes.
- Attach long pieces of ribbon to the stars.
- They are shooting stars.
- Throw them in the air across the room.
- Make at least four, so you can put on a Wish Upon a Star show, by throwing them one after the other.
- Repeat.

Things you could invite your child/adult to do

- Watch you throw the stars.
- Say, "throw," "star" or any version of that.
- Pick up the stars and give to you to throw them again.
- Throw the stars themselves.
- Make the stars with you.
- Make a wish before they throw the stars.

FLOATY WAVY SCARF GAME

- Get a thin silk scarf or a sari.
- Lay it out on the floor.
- Take one side and make it ripple like a wave.
- Repeat.

Other things you could do with the silk scarf

- Throw it up in the air so it floats down to the ground.
- Have your child/adult lie down on the floor and drop the scarf, so it gently floats down and lands on them.
- Wave it over them so that it touches them a little and then you pull it up again and let it wave down and touch them slightly again before you pull it away. Keep repeating this.

- Hold it as if you are bull fighting, but the bull is your child/adult and they run through it feeling the scarf on their face.

Things you could invite your child/adult to do

- Watch the scarf fall and ripple like a wave.
- Lie down so that you can wave or drop the scarf on them.
- Say, "scarf," "wave" or "down," or any version of that.
- Look at you to indicate that they are ready for you to drop the scarf.
- Drop the scarf on you.
- Make the scarf ripple and wave.
- Point to which scarf they want you to drop.
- Tell you which scarf they want you to use.

HOT WHEELS RACE OF THE CENTURY GAME

- Line up every toy vehicle you have that has wheels.
- Slide them one by one across the room.
- Which one goes the furthest?
- Which one goes the slowest?
- Roll them quickly one after the other.
- Roll three at a time.
- Roll two at a time
- If you have a slide, roll them down a slide.
- Make a ramp out of a cardboard box and roll them down the ramp and see how far they get.

Things you could invite your child/adult to do

- Watch you roll the cars.
- Give you the cars they want you to roll.
- Declare the winner.
- Tell you how many to race at one time.
- Say, "roll," "car" or any version of that.
- Look at you to indicate that they are ready for you to roll the cars.

SUPERFACT IT

RESEARCH INTERESTING FACTS ABOUT THINGS THAT SPIN OR STRING/RIBBON

Here are some topics to inspire your research:

- How many machines require a spinning mechanism to function?
- How did the wheel change the world?
- How fast can you spin something?
- Who invented the wheel?
- How do you make something that electronically spins?
- How do you make a rotating fan?
- How many parts of a vehicle require a spinning/propeller-like mechanism?
- Does the human body have a similar mechanism?
- Where can you find propellers and spinning systems already in nature?
- How many machines do you have in your house that use a spinning mechanism?
- How many knots can you tie in a piece of string and what are their names and uses?
- Do any sports involve things that spin, dangle or drop? Find facts about rhythmic gymnastics competitions.
- Why was ribbon first invented?

How you can use this information with your child/adult

Share it with your child/adult

- Have a discussion together about spinning machines, ribbon or string.
- Ask what other information or facts they would be curious to know about wheels/spinning mechanisms and propellers, string or ribbon.

- Show them pictures of the wheels, spinning mechanisms and propellers, ribbon gymnastics or knots you are talking about. Read them sections from instruction manuals.
- Share your thoughts and opinions on the information you found. Do you think it is interesting? What kind of spinning mechanism would you like to invent? Could you be a rhythmic gymnast with a ribbon? How many knots can you tie?

Make your own propeller

- Type "How to make a propeller using an old CD" or "How to make a propeller at home" into an internet search engine and you will come up with lots of short videos on how to do that. Choose one that suits your situation and child/adult.
- Have fun together making a real propeller that works!

Spinning Olympics

- Make a list of some made-up "Olympic" spinning events that you or your child/adult could enter. Here are some ideas for inspiration:
  - Multiple spinning event: this is where you attempt to keep four objects spinning at the same time. The Olympic champion will be the person who manages to keep all four objects spinning the longest.
  - Hula hoop spin: how long can you keep a big hula hoop spinning before it falls over?
  - Hurdle spin: can you start a plate spinning then run a three-hurdle jump course and get back to the plate before it stops spinning?

Invent your own ideal fan or super wheel

- What would it be?
- Plan it out together.
- Make a blueprint drawing for your fan or wheel.
- Write out an instruction manual for it.

Weather

BE IT

VERSION 1

- Get a big poster board and draw a big cloud.
- Put it on the ground and sit on it.
- Get a box of tissues. Take out a tissue and tear it into little pieces to make snow.
- You are a snowstorm.

VERSION 2

- Get a blanket/throw and swirl it like a lasso above your head and around your body.
- Move around the room in circles while lassoing the blanket.
- You are a typhoon or a hurricane.

VERSION 3

- On a piece of paper write, "Weather Channel."
- Underneath, draw buttons that say:
  - "Press here for today's weather"
  - "Press here for tomorrow's weather"
  - "Press here for the ten-day forecast"

> – "Press to enter your zip code or town for weather in your area."
> • You are a human weather channel.

Abracadabra! Three different ways to become the weather!

Things you can do once you have become the weather

Version 1

- Throw the snow all over the room—in the air, on you and your child/adult.
- Get a bunch of stuffed animals, or cars, and have the snow-storm only fall on them.
- Get an umbrella and put it up to protect yourself from the snow.
- Sing, "I am dancing in the snow" to the tune of "Singin' in the Rain." As you sing, dance around and throw the snow in the air.
- Sing, "Snowflakes are falling on my head" to the tune of "Rain-drops keep falling on my head" and make them fall on your head. Then, "Snow drops are falling on my toes" and make them fall on your toes. Do it on your child/adult's head and toes. Do different body parts, one by one.

Version 2

- Make the swirling/howling sounds of a typhoon or hurricane.
- Have fun bumping into things and knocking them down in a fun, slapstick way.
- Build a tower out of boxes or blocks, then become the typhoon/hurricane that knocks them over.

Version 3

- Press the button and declare in a "presenter's voice" what the day's weather will be. Then do the same for tomorrow's weather, and continue through the days of the week.
- You can make more buttons for the weather in America and Africa and in the houses of people you know.

- Make up a new type of weather. For inspiration, you could say:
  - "Tomorrow it will be raining the alphabet. Our reporters are claiming that the rain has retired, and the alphabet will be taking over as of tomorrow. People everywhere are advised not to go out without their bike helmets."
  - "With great excitement, we announce that tomorrow the weather will get so cold that the clouds will produce sugar crystals. This, mixed with icicles, will produce ice pops instead of snow. Don't forget to leave the house with your appetite."

Things you could invite your child/adult to do

For Version 1

- Throw the snow with you.
- Pick up the snow and give to you to throw.
- Tell you which body part to throw the snow on next.
- Tell you where to throw the snow.
- Say, "snow" or "throw."
- Get animals or toys for you to drop the snow onto.
- Sit underneath the umbrella with you.
- Hold the umbrella.

For Version 2

- Pick up the blanket and give it to you to become the hurricane.
- Lasso the blanket with you to become a double force typhoon/ hurricane.
- Say, "hurricane," "typhoon" or "blow it down," or any version of those.
- Build the towers for you (the typhoon) to knock down.

For Version 3

- Come up with fun and different weathers.
- Watch you as you press the button and become the presenter.
- Press the buttons to hear you announce the weather.

- Draw a picture of the weather you announce.
- Become the weather station presenter.
- Act out the different weather.

MAKE IT/DRAW IT

WEATHER SYMBOLS GAME

- Print and cut out weather symbols—clouds, clouds with rain, rain, lightning, wind and sun. To do this, just type "weather symbols" into an internet search engine and you will find a whole bunch of them.
- You will need three of each symbol.
- Collect the following items:
  - A bag of cotton balls. These will be clouds.
  - Aluminum foil. Cut the foil into strips. Make at least six strips. This will be the lightning.
  - A water squirter—but not in the shape of a gun. This will be the rain.
  - A flashlight. This will be the sun.
  - A handheld paper fan, or something you can use as a fan. This will be the wind.
  - Sunglasses for when the sun comes out.
  - An umbrella to put up when it rains.
- Tape all the weather symbols to yourself.
- Pull one off, hold it up and say its name. Then, if it is the:
  - sun—shine the flashlight
  - cloud—throw some cotton balls in the air
  - rain—use the water squirter
  - lightning—make the sound of thunder and then throw the lightning tin foil strips into the air
  - wind—use the fan to create wind.
- Keep doing that until all the weather symbols have been done.
- Then stick them all back on and repeat.

Things you could invite your child/adult to do

- Pull off the symbol they want to see next.
- Say the symbol they want to see next.
- You take off a symbol, and they make the weather happen.
- They stick the symbols on themselves, and take them off, while you make the weather happen.
- Put up the umbrella when it rains.
- Run and take cover under a blanket when the thunder and lightning come.
- Run away from the rain.
- Sunbathe when the sun comes out.
- Put on the dark glasses when the sun comes out.

RAINBOW MAKER GAME

- Print out coloring pages of rainbows.
- Print out coloring pages of clouds and raindrops.
- Cut them out.
- Take the biggest rainbow coloring page you can print out and put it on the table.
- Take the symbol of a rain cloud and the sun and have them crash into one another.
- Once they have crashed, start singing the rainbow song "I can sing a rainbow." Here's a link to it if you do not know it: https://youtu.be/yLpEGM34Fic
- As you sing, start coloring in the rainbow.
- Color in one color strip and then crash the symbols together again and repeat, coloring in another.

Things you could invite your child/adult to do

- Color in the rainbow.
- Watch you color in the rainbow.
- Crash the sun and the rain together.
- Sing the rainbow song with you.
- Become a rainbow arch themselves.

- Say, "color rainbow."
- Give you the next color marker for the rainbow.
- Say, "crash sun and rain."

SHOWTIME IT

EARTHQUAKE DISASTER GAME

- Put a tablecloth or old sheet on the table or floor.
- On top of the sheet or tablecloth set a table with plastic knives, forks, plates, cups, plastic bottle and empty cereal and milk cartons.
- Put a hand on the ground and look attentive. Have a shocked expression on your face.
- Say, "I feel an earthquake coming."
- Shake the tablecloth just a little and then slowly increase the shaking until everything falls over or off the table.
- Put it all back and do it again. Do it as many times as your child/adult is interested.
- Variation: Build tall houses out of empty cardboard boxes on the tablecloth or sheet.

Things you could invite your child/adult to do

- Set the table again after the earthquake happens.
- Build up the houses and towers after the earthquake happens.
- Shake the tablecloth or sheet with you.
- Put their hands on the floor/table and feel the earthquake coming.
- Say, "An earthquake is coming."
- Make the earthquake happen by shaking the tablecloth or sheet.

SOUND OF WEATHER MUSIC CONCERT

- Bang drums. (Drums can be upside-down buckets or pots and pans.) Bang these as loudly as you can for thunder. And then very quietly and gently in a "pitter patter" rhythm for rain.
- "Ting" a triangle for the "sound" of snow.
- Blow down a plastic tube to make the sound of wind, or make a tunnel with your fists and blow the "wooshhh" sound of the wind through them.
- Make bird chirping sounds to indicate a sunny day.
- Sing the name of the weather before you make its music.
- Sing the name and hold up a picture of the weather before you make its music.
- Keep interchanging between the different weather sounds for as long as your child/adult is interested.

Things you could invite your child/adult to do

- Give you the different instruments to play.
- Tell you the type of weather to play.
- Watch you play the different sounds.
- Give you the picture of the weather they want to play next.
- Blow through your hands to make the wind.
- Blow through their own hands to make the wind.
- "Ting" the triangle.
- Bang the drums as loud as they can.
- Make the "pitter patter" rhythm on the drums.
- Chirp like a bird in the sun.

WEATHER RIDE GAME

- Cut out a giant cloud shape from a big poster board. Put it on the ground.
- Get blue card and put it on the floor to symbolize a big puddle.

- Pick up your child and do a jumping floating dance with them in your arms on the cloud. If you have an adult, hold hands and jump from the cloud to the puddle and back again.
- Then put a rain hat on and hop and jump into the puddle and do a "splish splash" dance with your child/adult in your arms or holding your hands.
- Jump in between the cloud and the puddle a few times.
- Put your child down and then pick them up again (or let go hands with your adult and join hands again) and repeat.

Things you could invite your child/adult to do

- Be picked up by you.
- Hold hands and jump with you from the puddle to the cloud.
- Watch you dance on the floating cloud and puddle.
- Dance on the puddle.
- Stand on the cloud, stand on the puddle.
- Jump on the cloud or puddle.
- Say, "cloud," "puddle," "jump," "splash."
- Copy your "floaty" and "splish splash" dance moves.
- Make up their own dance moves.

SUPERFACT IT

RESEARCH INTERESTING FACTS ABOUT WEATHER

Here are some topics you can research for inspiration:

- How many different weather symbols are there?
- How do scientists predict the weather (i.e., how do they predict snow or rain or a storm or a hurricane or a tsunami)?
- How has climate change affected the weather in different countries?

- What are the names of the five biggest hurricanes or typhoons of the 21st century?
- What is a storm chaser?
- How many people get struck by lightning each year?
- Who has been struck by lightning the most times and survived?
- How did they predict the weather in the time of World War II?
- What instruments does a scientist use to predict the weather?
- Who is the most popular TV weather presenter today?
- TV weather presenters often have an individual gimmick or dress style. What are their gimmicks?
- Who are the most renowned and famous climatologists?
- How many different types of rain are there?
- What do the following mean when talking about weather:
  - Atmospheric pressure
  - Wind
  - Humidity
  - Precipitation?

How to use this information with your child/adult

Share it with your child/adult

- Have a discussion together about this interesting information.
- Ask them what other information and facts they would be curious to know about the weather.
- As you talk, show them pictures of all the weather symbols, scientists, weather stations and so on.
- Share your thoughts and opinions on the information you found. Do you think it is interesting? What is your most favorite climate to live in? To holiday in? If you could, would you eliminate a certain weather completely from the whole world? If so, which one? And what would it mean for the world if that weather did not exist?

Make a weather forecast show

- You both become a weather forecaster and put on a show. You could become your favorite one or the TV presenter you would like to be if you were one.
- What will be your TV outfit?
- What will be your gimmick?
- Create your map and symbols. Draw these on a poster board or print them out from the internet.
- Will you give the weekend forecast, or just tomorrow or a ten-day rolling forecast?
- Write and learn your lines.
- Present to each other or include other family members in the "audience."
- Variation: Interview each other about your career, expertise and style as a weather forecaster.

Weather Conditions Game

- Write down one type of weather on a piece of paper. Do this for as many types of weather as you can think of.
- Fold each piece of paper in half so that you cannot see what is written on it. Put them in a bowl.
- Each take turns taking out a piece of paper.
- Read aloud what is written on the piece of paper and then the game is to say all the atmospheric conditions that have to happen in order to make that type of weather. For example, precipitation falls as snow when the air temperature is below 2°C and when there is very little moisture in the air.
- When one person has finished saying everything they know, the other person gets to add anything that they might have missed out.

Sensory Hocus Pocus

SQUEEZES/MASSAGE

PUPPET SQUEEZES

- Take a puppet with a big mouth and squeeze your child/adult's hand.
- Intensify the pressure of the squeeze. (Remember, our children/adults often like deep pressure so do not be afraid to squeeze strongly.)
- As you intensify the pressure, look at your child/adult's face to make sure that they are enjoying the pressure.
- Release and move away to the other side of the room.
- Immediately come back towards your child/adult with the puppet, opening and closing the puppet's mouth with your hand.
- Give the other hand a squeeze.
- Repeat.
- Variations:
  - Do the same with their feet.
  - Squeeze in the same way all the way up their arms or legs.
  - Squeeze without a puppet, just using your hands.

Things you could invite your child/adult to do

- Put each hand in the puppet's mouth.
- Say, "squeeze."

- Say, "squeeze hand."
- Count how long they want you to squeeze their hand.
- Look at you moving away and towards them.
- Write the word "squeeze."
- Choose the puppet they want you to squeeze their hand with.

HEAD SQUEEZE GAME

Version 1

- Put your hand underneath your child/adult's chin and on top of their head and squeeze.
- Slowly increase the pressure while you are looking to make sure they are enjoying this pressure.
- Release and then squeeze again.
- Repeat for as long as your child/adult is motivated.

Version 2

- Put your hands either side of their head (by the temple) and squeeze your hands together.
- Slowly increase the pressure while you are looking to make sure they are enjoying this pressure.
- Release and then squeeze again.
- Repeat for as long as your child/adult is motivated.

Version 3

- Put your hand on their forehead and the other one on the back of their head and squeeze both hands together.
- Slowly increase the pressure while you are looking to make sure they are enjoying this pressure.
- Release and then squeeze again.
- Repeat for as long as your child/adult is motivated.

Things you could invite your child/adult to do in all the head-squeezing games

- Lean in and give you their head to squeeze.
- Look at you to indicate they want another head squeeze.
- Say, "squeeze" or "squeeze head."
- Put your hand on the part of the head they want you to squeeze.

LOTION MASSAGE GAME

Version 1

- Get an organic, gluten-free and fragrance-free lotion.
- Put a little on your hand then massage your child/adult's hand.
- Press your thumbs and fingers into their hand with confidence.
- Keep checking to make sure that they are enjoying the pressure.
- Stop and do the same with the other hand.
- Repeat.
- Variation: Do the same with their feet.

Version 2

- Get an organic, gluten-free and fragrance-free lotion.
- Put a little on your hand then massage your child/adult's arms.
- Use long confident strokes from the shoulder to the wrist.
- Do five on one arm.
- Then do five long strokes on the other arm.
- Repeat.
- Variation: Do the same for legs, with strokes from the knee to the ankle.

Things you could invite your child/adult to do in both lotion massage games

- Give you their hand, foot, arm or leg for you to massage.
- Squeeze the lotion onto your hand.
- Give you the lotion bottle.
- Look at you to indicate that they want you to massage them.
- Say, "massage," "massage arm" and so on.

THERAPY BALL DEEP PRESSURE GAME

- Have your child/adult lie down on the floor, either on their front or back.
- Get a big therapy ball.
- Roll it over them.
- Roll it over them again, this time pushing down on the ball a little so that it puts more pressure on their body.
- Do it again, this time adding more pressure.
- Keep rolling it over them adding more and more pressure. (You can use your whole body to create more pressure.)
- As you do this, keep checking with them either verbally or by observing their body cues to make sure that they are enjoying this pressure.
- Keep doing this for as long as they are motivated for it.
- Variation: Isolate one part of their body, like the hand, arm or leg, and just do that part.

Things you could invite your child/adult to do

- Take the ball and put it on their body for you to begin.
- Give you the ball for you to roll on their body.
- Look at you to indicate they want to roll the ball over them.
- Point to which part of their body they want you to roll the ball over.
- Say, "roll" or "roll ball."

CLAPPING/TAPPING

HAND CLAPPING GAME

- Put your child/adult's hand between your two hands.
- Clap your hands together so each of your hands claps either side of your child/adult's hand. (This give the same kind of sensory input that your child/adult gives to themselves when they are clapping their hands together or slapping the sides of their bodies or the floor or wall.)
- While you clap your hands, do a few in a row in a clear rhythmical pattern. It is always important to do the claps in a steady rhythm, as this adds to the sensory experience. It feels better and helps your child/adult know what to expect.
- Pause and repeat for as long as they are motivated by the game.
- Variation: Do the same clapping all the way up their arms to their shoulders and down again.

Things you could invite your child/adult to do

- Take your hands and put them on the body part they want you to clap.
- Give you their arm or hand to clap.
- Look at you to indicate that they want you to clap their hands or arm more.
- Say, "clap," "hand" or "clap hand/arm."

FOOT CLAPPING GAME

- With your child/adult sitting on the floor or in a chair, pick up their foot and tap/clap the bottom of their sole in a rhythmical pattern. Do this maybe ten times in a row. Pause and do it again. (This gives them a similar feeling that stomping and banging their

feet on the floor does, as well as the sensation that bouncing on a trampoline gives to the bottom of their feet.)
- Do the same thing with the other foot.
- Variations:
  - As you tap/clap the bottom of their feet, do it to the rhythm of a song they know and sing that song.
  - Do the same clapping all the way up their leg to their knee and down again.

Things you could invite your child/adult to do

- Take your hands and put them on the body part they want you to clap.
- Give you their foot or leg to clap.
- Look at you to indicate that they want you to clap their foot or leg.
- Say, "clap," "foot" or "clap foot/leg."
- Sing the song with you.
- Hum in rhythm with the song.
- Tell you the number of claps they want or the song they want.

TAPPING THE MOUTH AND JAW GAME

Version 1

- Use just your index finger and middle finger on each hand.
- Put those fingers on your child/adult's mouth and tap them outwards from the center of their mouth along their jaw to their ear and then back again, and then on the opposite side.
- Make sure you keep a good, steady, fast rhythm going.
- Repeat for as long as they are motivated.

Version 2

- Use just your index finger and middle finger on each hand.
- Using each hand, alternately tap in the center of their mouth.
- Make sure you keep a good, steady, fast rhythm going.
- Repeat for as long as they are motivated.

Version 3

- Use just your index finger and middle finger on one hand.
- Tap the whole area of your child/adult's mouth and chin. Make sure the whole of your fingers give sensory input to their mouth and chin area.
- Make sure you keep a good, steady, fast rhythm going along the mouth area and back again.
- Repeat for as long as they are motivated.

Version 4

- Use just the tips of your index finger and middle finger on one hand.
- With your fingertips tap the whole area around your child/adult's lips, tapping just the skin area not the lips themselves.
- Make sure you keep a good, steady, fast rhythm going.
- Repeat for as long as they are motivated.

Things you could invite your child/adult to do

- Take your fingers and put them where they want you to tap.
- Look at you to indicate they want more taps.
- Lean their face forward to indicate they want you to tap.
- Say, "tap," "mouth," "chin," "tap mouth."

SWINGING/SPINNING

SWING GAME

Version 1

- If your child is small enough, scoop your arms under their armpits and around their chest and swing them from side to side.
- As you do this, you can sing the word "swing."
- Put them down and repeat for as long as they are motivated.
- Variations:
  - You could swing them fast or slow.
  - You could swing them while slightly shaking them—a "shaky swing."
  - You could give them a "monkey swing" or a "pig swing" or a "dog swing," making that animal sound.
  - You could swing them from side to side while counting up to ten and then on the tenth one let go and throw them (safely) onto a crash mat or bed.
  - Do the same as above but instead of swinging them from side to side you spin them in a full circle, round and round.

Version 2

- If your child is small enough, have them lie down on the floor and take hold of their feet.
- Pick them up by their feet so that they are upside-down. (*If you are trying this for the first time with your child, make sure you do this slowly and check in to make sure that they are okay with being upside-down.*)
- While you are holding them upside-down by their feet, swing them from side to side.
- Say the words "swing upside-down" as you swing them.
- Variation: Spin your child by their feet in a full circle.

Version 3

- If your child is small enough, cradle them in your arms like a baby.
- Swing them back and forth in your arms.
- You can use the word "swing" as you do that.
- You could sing a lullaby as you swing them.
- Variation: Do the same as above but instead of swinging you spin in a full circle, round and round.

Version 4

- If your child is small enough, pick them up so their legs are straddled around you and their face is facing your face.
- Dip them down so they are upside-down and their head is by your knees.
- Flip them up again.
- Repeat for as long as they are motivated.
- Variation: Instead of flipping them up and down, spin them in a full circle.

Things you could invite your child to do

- Back into you to indicate they want another swing.
- Give you their feet to indicate they want an upside-down swing.
- Lift their arms up to indicate they want you to pick them up and give them a cradle swing.
- Say, "swing," "swing me," swing fast," swing slow," "cradle swing," "monkey swing," "upside-down swing," "shaky swing," "up," "down" or any other version (or "spin" for the variations).
- Look at you to indicate they want another swing.
- Write the word swing/spin.
- Point to the word swing/spin.

SWING IN A HAMMOCK GAME

- This is great for an older child/adult.
- Put up a hammock in your house. (You don't have to buy a hammock; you can use a sheet, blanket or sari.)
- Invite them to hop into the hammock and swing them from side to side.

Things you could invite your child/adult to do

- Get in the hammock.
- Help you put up the hammock.
- Put a soft toy in the hammock.
- Say, "swing" or "swing hammock."
- Swing you in the hammock.

FULL BODY INPUT

CRASH MAT GAME

- If your child is small enough, pick them up and run around the room with them.
- As you are running around the room you could say something like, "Whoa, Whoa, we are going to crash."
- Then with great anticipation, stop by the crash mat (or bed) and throw them down onto it.
- Variations: While you are running around the room with your child in your arms you could:
  - spell out loud the word "crash." Once you have spelt it, then you throw them down
  - count down from ten and throw them once you get to zero
  - once they have crashed on the mat, crash other soft toys on top of them. The more the merrier.

Things you could invite your child to do

- Lift up their arms to indicate they want you to pick them up and crash them again.
- Look at you to indicate they want another crash.
- Say, "crash," "crash me," "crash hard" or "crash me now."
- Spell out the word "crash" with you.
- Count down to zero with you.
- Tell you which stuffed animal to throw down on top of them.

WRAP UP BLANKET GAME

- Put a blanket or sheet on the floor.
- Invite your child/adult to lie down on the blanket/sheet.
- Wrap one side of the blanket over their body and tuck it around one side of them.
- Roll them so that they are tightly rolled up in the blanket like a hot dog.
- Once they are tightly wrapped up in the blanket/sheet, pull the open side of the blanket so they quickly roll out of it.
- Repeat for as long as they are motivated to continue.

Things you could invite your child/adult to do

- Lie on the blanket/sheet.
- Say, "roll" or "roll me."
- Look at you to indicate that they want to be rolled up or rolled out.
- Try to roll you up in the blanket.

PERPETUAL MOTION: RIDES

Rides are great because they give our children/adults a full body experience. They are also great for those who like to be in perpetual motion, as a ride can provide that too. For bigger children or adults, see the "Blanket Ride Game" and the "Office Chair Ride Game." If your child is smaller, all the ride games will work for you.

PIGGYBACK RIDE GAME VERSION 1

- Invite your child to hop on your back.
- Move around the room at a trot so that your child gets a little bit of a bounce.
- Do this for a minute or two then put your child down on the ground.
- Repeat as many times as they are motivated.

PIGGYBACK RIDE GAME VERSION 2

- Invite your child to hop on your back.
- Move around the room at a fast trot while singing your child's favorite song or nursery rhyme. If you do not know what that is, sing this one:
    I'm a little donkey, ee-or! ee-or!
    I'm a little donkey, ee-or! ee-or!
    I clip, clip clop till my feet get sore.
    Everyone say, ee-or!
- Do this for a minute or two then put your child down on the ground.
- Repeat as many times as they are motivated.

PIGGYBACK RIDE GAME VERSION 3

- Invite your child to hop on your back.
- Remind your child to hang on tight.
- Move around the room in big wide zig-zags. As you zig or zag, do so in an exaggerated way, so your child gets moved around from side to side.

- Do this for a minute or two then put your child down on the ground.
- Repeat as many times as they are motivated.

PIGGYBACK RIDE GAME VERSION 4

- Print out five pictures of little puppy dogs.
- Print out one picture of a grown-up "mommy" dog.
- Stick the mommy dog picture on the table. Stick the other little puppy dogs around the room on different walls at the height your child will be on your back.
- Invite your child to hop on your back.
- Move around the room at a trot. Trot over to one of the puppy dogs, take the picture down and tell your child that you are rescuing the puppies and taking them back to their mommy. Then trot over to the table and put the puppy with the mommy on the table.
- Do the same with all the puppy dogs.
- Do this until all the puppies are with their mommy.
- Repeat the game as many times as your child is motivated.
- Variations:
  - Do the same thing with any animal. You can also do it with numbers or letters that spell a particular word. Or you can do it with literally anything that you think your child would like.
  - Put up different pictures of animals and when you trot over to each one, point and touch the picture or say the name of the animal and then make the animal sound.

PIGGYBACK RIDE GAME VERSION 5

- Put up a basketball hoop on the top of a door or on the wall. (If you do not have a basketball hoop, just use a bucket and put it up on a table.)
- Invite your child to hop on your back.
- Get a ball.
- Run around the room five times with your child on your back while bouncing the basketball.
- After the fifth round, stop and shoot a hoop. Cheer yourself when you get it in.
- Repeat as many times as your child is motivated. For this game, you can keep your child on your back the whole time.

PIGGYBACK RIDE GAME VERSION 6

- Position a drum on a table on one side of the room.
- Invite your child to hop on your back.
- Move around the room at a trot so that your child gets a little bit of a bounce.
- Stop at the drum and bang it at the rhythm of a horse trot.
- Resume trotting around the room.
- Stop at the drum and bang it again in the rhythm of a horse trot.
- Repeat as many times as your child is motivated.
- Variation: Do the same thing with any musical instrument; it could be a triangle, a penny whistle, harmonica or a little piano.

Things you could invite your child to do in the piggyback ride games

- Get on your back.
- Hold on so they do not fall off.
- Look at you to indicate that they want the ride to continue. (If your child is on your back you can position yourself in front of a

mirror and ask them to look at you through the mirror. This may be a little easier for you and for them to look at you.)

- Lift their arms up towards you to be picked up for another piggyback ride.
- Say, "piggyback," "ride," "want ride," "zig-zag piggyback," "fast piggyback," "bouncy piggyback," "get puppy," "get letter E," or make any animal sound (or any version of words that makes sense for the version of piggyback ride you are playing).
- Look at the picture on the wall.
- Pull a picture off the wall and put it with the "mommy" dog.
- Point to the picture.
- Tap on the picture.
- Decide what animals you are going to save.
- Decide what word you are going to spell.
- Shoot a hoop.
- Help you keep count of how many basketball hoops you each score.
- Play the musical instrument.

RIDE ON A BLANKET GAME

This is great if your child is bigger and/or you are not able to pick them up.
- Put a blanket on the floor.
- Invite your child to sit on it.
- Pull the blanket around the room.
- Do this for a minute.
- Stop.
- Repeat as many times as you want.
- Variations:
  - Gather up a lot of the blanket with your child sitting in the middle, then move it around in a circle so that your child gets a spin while you stay standing in one spot. You can get quite a speed going.
  - Add in the exact same variations of the piggyback rides above. You are just doing them with your child having a ride on a blanket instead of on your back.

Things you could invite your child to do

- Sit on the blanket.
- Look at you to indicate they want you to give them a ride.
- Say, "pull," "pull me," "blanket ride," "ride," "spin," "spin me."
- Point to where they want you to move them.
- Anything from the "Things you could invite your child to do" section for the piggyback ride variations.

OFFICE CHAIR RIDE VERSION 1

This is great for a teenager or adult.
- Use a chair that has wheels and spins around through 360 degrees, like an office chair.
- Invite your child/adult to sit on the chair.
- Spin it around.
- Do this for a minute.
- Stop the spinning.
- Repeat for as long as they are motivated.
- Variation: Push them on the chair around the room.

OFFICE CHAIR RIDE VERSION 2

This is great for a teenager or adult.
- Use a chair with wheels.
- Invite your child/adult to sit on the chair.
- Set up musical stations around the room. In one corner there is a drum, the other corner a harmonica, another corner a tambourine. (Use any instrument that you have.)
- Push your child/adult in the chair to each station and play the instrument and then move on to the next musical station, play that instrument and so on.
- Repeat for as long as they are motivated.
- Variations:
  - Instead of musical stations, have story sections, with

a page of an article or story at each one. You read
part of the article or story at each stop.
- Have anything else you can think of that your child/
adult may find interesting at each section. (You might
find some inspiration in the "Superfact it" sections of
the games for other motivations.)

Things you could invite your child/adult to do

- Sit on the chair.
- Look at you to indicate that they want another spin or ride.
- Say, "spin," "push," "move," "play drum," "music."
- Invite them to play the musical instrument themselves.
- Give you a spin or a push in the office chair.
- Read the part of the story that is at that station.
- Decide what it is they want to have in the corner stations.

HURDLES, JUMPS AND RUNNING

These can be fun for all children/adults, but particularly for those
who like to run from one wall to the other wall, pace, climb and are
in constant motion.

HURDLE GAME

- Create some little hurdle jumps. Create two little
"towers" of blocks or books at least 3 feet apart.
Balance a stick or a long thin piece of cardboard
between them. Make the height really easy for your
child/adult to jump over first.
- Create as many as your room allows.
- Then run and jump over them.
- Hop and hop over them.
- Skip and skip over them.
- Stop and adjust the height of the hurdles to make it a
little bit more challenging.

- Repeat the jump, hop and skip sequence.
- Stop and adjust the height of the hurdles to make it a little bit more challenging.
- Keep repeating for as long as your child/adult is motivated.
- Variations:
  - Create each hurdle to be at a different height.
  - Paint your faces and dress up as if you were horses or professional show jumpers and pretend it is a big show jumping event.
  - Pretend you are famous Olympic hurdlers. Everyone gets a medal at the end.

Things you could invite your child/adult to do

- Watch you do the hurdle course.
- Run and jump the hurdles.
- Skip and skip over the hurdles.
- Hop and hop over the hurdles.
- Adjust the heights with you.
- Take turns running the course.
- Cheer you as you attempt to do the hurdle course.
- Design more and different hurdle courses to attempt.
- Dress up as a horse or professional show jumper.
- Dress up as an Olympian.
- Give out medals.
- Create medals for the participants.
- Time how long it takes you to complete the course.

HIGH JUMP GAME

- Create one jump. Create two little "towers" of blocks or books at least 3 feet apart. Balance a stick or a long thin piece of cardboard between them. Make the height really easy for your child/adult to jump over first.

- Stand in front of it and jump over it.
- Then make it a little higher.
- Stand in front of it and jump over that.
- Make it as high as you can jump over.
- Take a running jump at it, if it helps you clear the jump.
- The game is to make it to your personal best height.

Things you could invite your child/adult to do

- Watch you do the high jump.
- Make the jump higher for you or for them.
- Cheer you as you attempt to jump a jump.
- Challenge themselves to do the jumps.
- Take turns with you, each jumping the same height.
- Say, "make it higher," "higher" or "jump."
- Say, "on your marks, get set, go" to help you know when to start the course.

LONG JUMP GAME

- Make a line on the floor with some artist tape.
- Then run up to it and see how far you can jump.
- Once you land, put a piece of artist tape down to measure how far you went.
- Keep trying to beat your personal best.

Things you could invite your child/adult to do

- Put the tape on the floor.
- Attempt the long jump themselves.
- Cheer you when you attempt the long jump.
- Say, "jump now."

SLALOM RUNNING COURSE

- Create a slalom running course.
- Put up towers of blocks in the following way:
  - Build a tower of blocks.
  - Build another tower of blocks three paces in front of the first tower and slightly to the right.
  - Build another tower three paces ahead of the last tower and to its left, in a straight line from the first one.
  - Then build another tower three paces ahead to the right of the last tower, in a straight line from the second tower.
  - Continue in this way until you have done the whole length of your room.
- The game is to run around each of the towers as fast as you can without knocking them down.
- Variations:
  - Create the towers in any pattern that you want; they could go in a full circle.
  - Use a stopwatch to time yourselves and write the times on a piece of paper you stick to the wall. You are trying to beat your personal best.

Things you could invite your child/adult to do

- Watch you run the course.
- Build or rebuild the towers with you.
- Run the course with you.
- Time you with a stopwatch.
- Write down your or their time on a piece of paper.
- Cheer you when you have finished running the course.
- Say, "on your marks, get set, go."
- Give you water after you have run the course.
- Try to beat their own personal best.

BOUNCING

Bouncing on a trampoline or on a therapy ball is something that some of our children/adults on the spectrum love to do. I have worked with many a child/adult whose main motivation was to bounce themselves on a therapy ball. If they were not bouncing on a trampoline or therapy ball, they were jumping on the floor or bouncing themselves in a kneeling position on the floor. In the sensory world, bouncing as well as swinging stimulates the vestibular sensory system. Our children and adults are in some sense giving themselves their own occupational therapy. We don't want to stop that; let's help them with it and at the same time strengthen their interactive and social skills. We can do that by including ourselves, using the simple games below.

THERAPY BALL GAME

Version 1: For a younger child

- Sit on a therapy ball yourself.
- Invite your child to sit on your lap.
- Bounce up and down for a minute.
- Stop bouncing; be completely still for a few seconds.
- Start bouncing again.
- Repeat for as long as your child is motivated.
- Variations:
  - Spell out the letters of the word "bounce" as you bounce.
  - Sing your child's favorite song as you bounce.

Version 2: For a younger child, with variations for an older child or adult

- Get some artist tape and tape a big box shape on the floor.
- Make the box shape as big as the room allows.
- Get the therapy ball and put it on the line of the square shape you have just made on the floor.

- Then bouncing and using your feet to propel yourself forward, bounce along the line in the shape of the square.
- Invite your child to sit on your lap.
- Start bouncing along the lines of the square shape with your child on your lap.
- Keep bouncing around the square for as long as your child/adult is motivated.
- Variations:
  - Draw an X shape, or a triangle shape or a smiley face with the artist tape. Or anything else you think your child will enjoy.
  - You can do this game with an older child or adult too. The only difference is you would each take turns bouncing on the ball around the shape on your own instead of being together on the same therapy ball. Have fun seeing if you can keep to the tape line without veering off to the left or right.

Version 3: For a child or adult

- Have your child/adult sit on the therapy ball.
- Stand behind them and hook your arms under their armpits and around their chest.
- Start bouncing them up and down.
- The idea here is you can bounce them higher than they can bounce themselves on their own. This gives you a role in the game.
- Bounce them for a minute, then stop.
- Then start bouncing them again for another minute, then stop for at least ten seconds.
- Repeat for as long as your child/adult is motivated.
- Variation: If your child needs more support you can actually sit behind them on the ball itself.

Things you could invite your child/adult to do in the therapy ball games

- Watch you bounce on the therapy ball around the square shape.
- Look at you to indicate they want you to bounce them again.
- Sit on your lap so that you can bounce them.
- Put your arms around them to indicate they want you to bounce them again.
- Help you make a shape out of artist tape on the floor.
- Suggest a shape for you to both bounce around.
- Say, "bounce," "bounce high," "bounce along the square."
- Tell you how many bounces they want you to bounce.
- Count with you as you bounce and count.
- Sing the song with you.

Appendix

Discover your child/adult's motivations

Spend 15 minutes a day for five days just observing your child/adult as they play by themselves. Notice not just what they are playing with but how they are playing with it. What senses are they predominantly using? As you observe them, notice what they are doing; if they are tapping things with their fingers, then that is their motivation. It does not have to be playing with something in the traditional sense. Our children play and explore differently. The following list will help you observe in a particular way. Just tick the boxes that are relevant to your child.

He touches or taps things in a rhythmic way.

☐ The rhythm is fast.
☐ The rhythm is slow.
☐ The rhythm is staccato.
☐ The rhythm is syncopated.

Add your child/adult's rhythm on the lines provided below.

....

....

....

....

....

She is visually stimulated.

☐ She looks at things out of the corner of her eye.
☐ She lines things up in neat rows.
☐ She likes to arrange things in scenes.
☐ She likes to arrange things in piles.
☐ She stares at the wall or ceiling, or at the woodwork or light switches.
☐ She stares intently at her own fingers as she slowly wiggles
☐ them.
☐ She looks at patterns while running her fingers over the
☐ pattern.
☐ She will watch the credits roll down the TV again and again.
☐ She will draw.
☐ She likes to watch the chalk dust fall.
☐ She watches things that move like fans or any electrical equipment.
☐ She stares at light on floorboards.
☐ She watches little things falling through the air like rice.
☐ She watches a scarf fall through the air.
☐ She closely watches the wheels of a car spin.
☐ She watches a piece of string dangle.
☐ She waves a belt along the floor, watching it move like a
☐ snake.

Add what your child/adult watches and how on the lines provided below.

....
....
....
....
....

He likes to engage in physical activities.

- ☐ He runs from one side of the room to another, banging his hands onto the walls.
- ☐ He paces using large steps, starting slowly and gathering speed, and then slowing down and again gathering speed.
- ☐ He flaps his hands, stimulating mainly his wrists.
- ☐ He flaps his fingers only.
- ☐ He shakes his head from side to side.
- ☐ He pushes his tongue against the side of his cheeks.
- ☐ He chews on any object he has.
- ☐ He slaps the side of his head and legs, or claps his hands.
- ☐ He jumps.
- ☐ He is constantly in motion.
- ☐ He holds an object most of the time.

Add your child/adult's particular physical activity on the lines provided below.

....

....

....

....

....

She likes to listen to sounds.

- ☐ She puts a car up close to her ear and listens to the whirl of the car wheels.
- ☐ She makes sounds to herself as she jumps, spins or watches things fall.
- ☐ She listens to the clank of a belt buckle falling to the ground as she watches it fall.
- ☐ She bangs doors, listening to the click of the door handle opening or closing.
- ☐ She says the same phrase or word over and over again, with a particular inflection or rhythm.
- ☐ She shakes bells.

Add the specific sound your child/adult likes to hear on the lines below.

....

....

....

....

....

He likes patterns.

- ☐ He likes to do puzzles.
- ☐ He likes numbers.
- ☐ He likes to spell words.
- ☐ He likes to solve math problems.

On the lines below write your child/adult's own specific interest in patterns.

....

....

....

....

....

She likes to engage with textures and touch.

- ☐ She loves soft things.
- ☐ She loves hard and bumpy textures.
- ☐ She loves furry things.
- ☐ She likes sandpaper.
- ☐ She will wrap herself up in a blanket.
- ☐ She loves silky cloths.
- ☐ She will roll cars up and down her arms.
- ☐ She likes soft touch.
- ☐ She likes hard pressure like squeezes.
- ☐ She loves ribbon.
- ☐ She loves the feel of hair.

On the lines below write any other texture or touch your child/adult likes.

....

....

....

....

....

What kind of spaces does he like?

- ☐ He likes the doors and windows to be open.
- ☐ He will always close the door.
- ☐ He will surround himself with cushions.
- ☐ He will play underneath the table, or in a small play tent or play house.
- ☐ He will play surrounded by a fortress of books or stuffed animals.
- ☐ He likes to play in a dark space.
- ☐ He likes to play in a light space.

On the lines provided below write down any other kind of space your child/adult enjoys.

....

....

....

....

....

What type of characters does she like?

- ☐ She likes plastic Disney characters.
- ☐ She likes soft, plush Disney characters.
- ☐ She likes movie characters.
- ☐ She likes characters from a storybook.

Write your child/adult's favorite characters on the lines provided below.

....

....

....

....

....

What music or song does your child/adult like?

Write them down on the lines provided below.

....

....

....

....

....

Does your child/adult show you a color preference?

If so, write them down on the lines provided below.

....

....

....

....

....

This time notice how your child/adult responds to what you do. As you read the list below, see if your child/adult likes you to do any of the actions. If you are not sure, then find out by trying the action with your child/adult. If they do, then that's their motivation.

- ☐ Speaking in funny voices, like Mickey Mouse and Donald Duck
- ☐ Using slapstick humor like pretending to fall on a banana skin
- ☐ Making big gestures, and big facial expressions
- ☐ Making big celebrations
- ☐ Singing to them
- ☐ Playing musical instruments
- ☐ Dancing in big and funny ways
- ☐ Whispering
- ☐ Using anticipation
- ☐ Talking softly
- ☐ Clapping hands
- ☐ Pretending to be an animal
- ☐ Reading books out loud
- ☐ Tickling them
- ☐ Giving big squeezes
- ☐ Blowing on their body.

Add any other things that you do that motivate your child/adult on the lines provided below.

....

....

....

....

....

....

....

....

Recommended Reading and Resources

Books

The Autism Language Launcher: A Parent's Guide to Helping Your Child Turn Sounds and Words into Simple Conversations by Kate C. Wilde

Autistic Logistics: A Parent's Guide to Tackling Bedtime, Toilet Training, Meltdowns, Hitting, and Other Everyday Challenges (second edition) by Kate C. Wilde

Autism Breakthrough: The Groundbreaking Method that Has Helped Families All Over the World by Raun K. Kaufman

Three books by Barry Neil Kaufman: *Son-Rise: The Miracle Continues, A Miracle to Believe In*, and *Happiness Is a Choice*

Websites

www.katecwilde.com

Kate's YouTube channel, Kate C. Wilde: www.youtube.com/channel/UCGqZboO0fRCpU3GK2X0oAHw

www.autismcrisisturnaround.com

https://autismtreatment.org

The Autism Treatment Center YouTube channel has hundreds of videos filled with creative ideas and games to help your child/adult on the autism spectrum. You can view them at: www.youtube.com/user/autismtreatment

The Son-Rise Program Online Course: https://online.autismtreatmentcenter.org

Specific resources to help with understanding red lights and joining

Pages 43–56 in *The Autism Language Launcher: A Parent's Guide to Helping Your Child Turn Sounds and Words into Simple Conversation* by Kate C. Wilde

Chapter 2 in *Autism Breakthrough: The Groundbreaking Method that Has Helped Families All Over the World* by Raun K. Kaufman

YouTube: https://youtu.be/WXGG6AME3Jo

Specific resources to help you understand what your child can understand even if they have not yet verbally communicated with you

Chapter 5, "Talk to Your Child: The Power of the Explanation" in *Autistic Logistics: A Parent's Guide to Tackling Bedtime, Toilet Training, Meltdowns, Hitting, and Other Everyday Challenges (second edition)* by Kate C. Wilde

Chapter 5, "The Power of What You Say to Your Child" in *The Autism Language Launcher: A Parent's Guide to Helping Your Child Turn Sounds and Words into Simple Conversations* by Kate C. Wilde